WHAT IS THAT PLANT?

This book is dedicated to all those who find joy and solace in gardens.

WHAT IS THAT PLANT?

A GUIDE TO IDENTIFYING 150 GARDEN PLANTS, WEEDS & WILDFLOWERS

LOUISE BURFITT

WHITE OWL

AN IMPRINT OF PEN & SWORD BOOKS LTD.
YORKSHIRE – PHILADELPHIA

First published in Great Britain in 2023 by
Pen and Sword WHITE OWL
An imprint of
Pen & Sword Books Ltd
Yorkshire - Philadelphia

ISBN 978 1 39900 616 3

A CIP catalogue record for this book is available from the British Library.

Typeset in 11 / 14 pts Cormorant Infant
by SJmagic DESIGN SERVICES, India.

Printed and bound in India by Replika Press Pvt. Ltd.

Pen & Sword Books Ltd incorporates the Imprints of Pen & Sword Books Archaeology, Atlas, Aviation, Battleground, Discovery, Family History, History, Maritime, Military, Naval, Politics, Railways, Select, Transport, True Crime, Fiction, Frontline Books, Leo Cooper, Praetorian Press, Seaforth Publishing, Wharncliffe and White Owl.

For a complete list of Pen & Sword titles please contact

PEN & SWORD BOOKS LIMITED
47 Church Street, Barnsley, South Yorkshire, S70 2AS, England
E-mail: enquiries@pen-and-sword.co.uk
Website: www.pen-and-sword.co.uk

or

PEN AND SWORD BOOKS
1950 Lawrence Rd, Havertown, PA 19083, USA
E-mail: Uspen-and-sword@casematepublishers.com
Website: www.penandswordbooks.com

Contents

Foreword

As a teenager, craving a creative outlet, I purchased a 35mm Pentax SLR at a car boot sale. I quickly became engrossed in the art of photography, snapping almost any scene I encountered – including many plants and flowers. After a sprawl of weeks spending every spare moment with my camera, I noticed something curious. The many hours I had spent looking through the viewfinder had taught me something. While my images were far from perfect, I could suddenly understand light. On the bus home from school, I'd stare at dappled sunshine winking through the trees, composing photographs in my mind almost without thinking. It was as if I could speak a new language, albeit one that I had been entirely unaware of before I had picked up a camera. I now understood how light behaved and I couldn't – nor did I want to – unsee it.

When, in my twenties, I started to take note of plants in more detail, I noticed a similar phenomenon. Walking around the garden with my grandfather had previously been an exercise in shrugging my shoulders when he asked me if I could name the plants he was pointing at, appreciating the shapes and colours of certain flowers nonetheless. But soon after I picked up my own trowel and started to garden, I found I could start to take an educated guess. The shapes of leaves had begun to look familiar to me, as I began to recognise how certain wildflowers and ornamental plants shared similar flower heads. I made a mental note of the way mint leaves and deadnettles looked alike. Later, with the help of the internet, I learned that they did in fact belong to the same plant family. Where once I'd been clueless as to the difference between – say – a chrysanthemum and a catmint, I now had a certain awareness of and relationship to plants, just like the one I had cultivated with light as a teenager.

Once you start looking – *really* looking – connections between different plants become apparent and identifying them becomes almost second nature. Of course, you won't get it right every time (and nor do you need to), but you'll soon be able to take a pretty good stab at it. Every outing turns into an opportunity to observe old favourites and discover new flowers previously unnoticed. Of course, knowing the name of something is not necessary to appreciate it – but in my experience, recognising the plants around me adds depth to my surroundings, bolstering my view that we are all part of a shared ecosystem and deepening my care towards the planet.

Sometimes people tell me, with a certain amount of shame for they know I love to garden, that they only know how to kill plants. They weren't born with a green thumb. I shake my head and admit that I used to think that way, too. I think of the late poet Mary Oliver when she wrote that to pay attention is our most vital and enduring work as humans. While she was referring to life more generally, I have come to adopt this as my unofficial motto when it comes to gardening. There's no such thing as a born gardener. No such thing as a convicted plant murderer. Paying attention is what matters, whether taking photographs of plants, identifying them or keeping them alive.

Introduction

How many times have you stood before a flower bed and thought to yourself, curious or exasperated, 'What *is* that plant?' Having a plot of soil to tend can be both a joy and a privilege, but it can also be maddening to stand before a tangle of leaves wondering what on earth you are looking at. Should I water that? Are those green shoots the seeds I carefully sowed and watered? Or are they weeds – itself a disputed term – that are also enjoying my care and attention?

If the abundance of apps that have sprung up to help would-be gardeners discern the plants at their feet is anything to go by, this is a common occurrence. Putting a name to something is often the beginning of a path towards understanding and as humans we are innately inquisitive beings, interested in and connected with our surroundings, both for evolutionary reasons and for the sake of sheer curiosity.

You don't need much to begin identifying plants. You don't even need a garden. Botanical field guides might recommend a magnifying glass, a pair of tweezers and a pocket encyclopaedia but while these things have their place, all you really need is an open mind. Plants are quite literally on our doorsteps, whether we have the luxury of our own outdoor space or not. All we need to do is notice them. I hope that the pages in this book will be a worthy and helpful companion in that endeavour.

Why identify plants?

Unless you're wandering around a botanical garden or browsing at a garden centre, plants don't tend to come with name tags. And given that there are more than 350,000 known plant species in the world, with many thousands of these found in the UK alone, the task of identifying what is growing outside your back door or in the hedgerow can be daunting.

Daunting, yes, but also important. Recognising the plants we're dealing with allows us to learn more about them. Once you know the name or family of a plant, you can start to understand its behaviour. And once you know a little about how it acts, you can get to grips with how best to take care of it. Identification is the first step in developing the skills to nurture the living beings we know as plants.

Even if you don't have a garden of your own, identifying plants in your nearby surroundings can still bring a great sense of satisfaction and belonging. The everyday is quickly transformed into a living field guide. Bus rides and weekend walks become new voyages in discovery, whatever your age or prior knowledge of botany. Spotting familiar favourites on the way to the shops rarely fails to bring a smile to my face. Plant identification can be a hobby in its own right, as well as a means to understanding more about the natural world and the planet we call home. In the face of the climate crisis, this feels more necessary than ever.

How to use this book

This book lists 150 common garden perennials, shrubs, trees, grasses, weeds and wildflowers that grow in the United Kingdom. It is designed to help allay that exasperating feeling you might feel staring, uncertain, at your soil. Each individual entry includes a detailed description and accompanying colour photograph. Details including leaf and flower colour and shape, toxicity and preferred location are included, aimed at aiding the identification process. At the back of the book, you'll find a glossary of common terms used in gardening that pop up throughout the book.

The individual plant entries are divided into four categories:

- Perennial plants & bulbs
  - Herbaceous plants with non-woody stems that return year after year
- Self-seeders & spreaders
  - Short-lived garden plants that drop their seed and return as new plants without human intervention
- Shrubs, grasses, trees & climbers
  - Woody bushes, ornamental grasses, climbing plants and trees that live for several or many years
- Weeds & wildflowers
  - Plants typically classified as weeds or those that grow in the wild

In each section, the plant entries are organised in alphabetical order.

Any encyclopaedia of common garden plants could sprawl for miles and miles, such is the diversity of plant life we're lucky enough to find here in Britain. With considerations such as length and usefulness to the reader in mind, I have chosen to omit annual plants that only grow for one short season and are therefore unlikely to recur and require identification. The exception to this rule is annuals that are classified as weeds or wildflowers (turn to p. 149) or that tend to self-seed or spread (see p. 55).

To use this book to its full potential, you might begin by asking yourself a series of questions to guide you on which chapter to start with when identifying an unknown plant. For example, you could ask yourself:

- Is it a woody plant, with branches all year round? (Turn to 'Shrubs, grasses, trees & climbers')
- Does it die back to ground level in the autumn? (Turn to 'Perennial plants & bulbs')
- Is it growing in between paving stones? (Turn to 'Weeds & wildflowers' or 'Self-seeders & spreaders')
- Are there lots of the same plant in a small area? (Turn to 'Self-seeders & spreaders')

These are just a handful of questions you might pose. From there, you can compare your plant's leaves, flowers, growing habits and more with the details in each individual entry, using the accompanying photographs to verify or exclude different options. Once correctly identified, the 'Perks' and 'Pitfalls' listings will help you decide how best to care for the plant and whether it deserves a place on your plot.

Guide to individual entries

Each individual plant entry is listed in the following format:

Plant common name (*Horticultural Latin name*)
Example: **Agapanthus** (*Agapanthus* spp.)

Flowers The main flowering period of the plant (this will vary by region).
Example: July to September

Foliage The leaves of the plant or tree, and whether they remain through winter (evergreen or semi-evergreen) or fall in autumn (deciduous).
Example: Deciduous

Height The plant's ultimate height.
Example: 1.2m

Spread The plant's ultimate horizontal spread.
Example: 50cm

Preferred conditions Does the plant prefer sun, shade or something in between?
Example: Sun

Origin Where the plant is believed to have first originated.
Example: South Africa

Toxicity Denotes whether toxic (and potentially fatal) effects on humans, cats, dogs or horses have been reported. While all care has been taken to verify this information, it is wise to always proceed with caution and keep animals and children away from unknown plants. Please note that even plants designated non-toxic can still cause unpleasant symptoms of gastrointestinal discomfort and pain if ingested.
Example: Toxic to humans, cats and dogs.

How to spot • Advice on how to identify the plant using attributes like colour, shape, size, and preferred location (such as sun or shade).
Example: Agapanthus have leaves that resemble those of spring bulbs.

Perks • A summary of the plant's positive attributes, whether beauty, longevity, flowering period or otherwise.
Example: The dried seed heads and leaves also provide winter interest if left on the plant.

Pitfalls • Does the plant have any major downsides? These will be summarised here and, where appropriate, I'll offer tips on how to remove the plant from your outdoor space. You won't find suggestions for chemical control in these pages as herbicides and weedkillers are generally damaging to wildlife and soil, but in extreme circumstances, their use can become necessary.
Example: If they are left outside in winter, they may refuse to flower the next year.

Did you know? • Here you'll find a piece of horticultural trivia related to the plant's name, location, habit, history or similar.
Example: Agapanthus like to have their roots restricted.

Author's note: Where no relevant information exists for an entry, it has been removed. Some plants, for example, have the potential to be so dangerous that listing their positive attributes seemed irresponsible, while others have no alternative names or do not produce flowers.

Perennial plants & bulbs

In many gardens and public spaces, perennials form the bulk of the plants on show. Perennial plants are those that return year after year, usually dying back completely over the winter months. The roots remain in the soil and re-emerge again in the spring. The technical definition of a perennial is any non-woody plant that lives for three or more years. For convenience, perennial flowering bulbs and corms, like daffodils (*Narcissus* spp.), are also included in this chapter.

Perennials are the largest group of plants and, as you'd expect from such a broad collection, there is incredible variety among them. Some prefer sun, others dappled or full shade. Select perennials flower in winter, but most of the popular British varieties bloom in spring, summer and autumn. Some – like perennial phlox (*Phlox paniculata*) – flower for almost three seasons, others – like peonies (*Paeonia* spp.) – for mere weeks. The perennial routine of dying back over winter means identification will usually only be possible for some of the year.

There are many thousands of perennial plants if you were to count all the various cultivars, and no book could include them all. This chapter selects some of the most popular and widely available perennial plants at the time of writing, as well as some personal favourites. May it act as a stepping stone to further perennial identification, for there are many, many more to find and recognise!

Agapanthus (*Agapanthus* spp.)

✴	**Flowers**	July to September
✴	**Foliage**	Deciduous
✴	**Height**	1.2m
✴	**Spread**	50cm
✴	**Preferred conditions**	Sun
✴	**Origin**	South Africa
✴	**Toxicity**	Toxic to humans, cats and dogs and cats
✴	**Also known as**	African lily, Lily of the Nile

Macie Jones   *Lisa Simenz Vera*

How to spot • Agapanthus have leaves that resemble those of spring bulbs – slender, strap-shaped, and a medium shade of green. The foliage forms large clumps at the base before sending up long green stems in July that produce striking spherical clusters of trumpet-shaped purple or white flowers.

Perks • Unlike some plants, they don't mind being grown in containers – in fact, they thrive in them. And their slim, slender profile means they can be grown at the front of a border or plot without blocking the view to plants behind. The dried seed heads and leaves also provide winter interest if left on the plant.

Pitfalls • If they are left outside in winters too cold and wet, plants may sulk and refuse to flower the next year. Therefore, many gardeners choose to grow them in pots, so they can be stored in warmer conditions over the colder months.

Did you know? • Agapanthus plants like to have their roots restricted. Crammed into a pot or under stress, they tend to flower best. Some gardeners advise only repotting them into a bigger container when the plant's roots crack open their original pot.

Alstroemeria (*Alstroemeria* spp.)

Author

Russell Moore

✳	**Flowers**	May to November
✳	**Foliage**	Deciduous
✳	**Height**	1m
✳	**Spread**	1m
✳	**Preferred conditions**	Sun
✳	**Origin**	South America
✳	**Toxicity**	No reported toxicity
✳	**Also known as**	Lily of the Incas, Peruvia lily

How to spot • A favourite of florists, you might recognise alstroemerias from their frequent presence in bouquets. The radiant flowers resemble lilies in shape and appearance, with bright streaks or spots at their throats. Colours range from pink to orange to white, purple and yellow, and often several of these on one flower. Leaves are blade-shaped and grow in intervals up the stems.

Perks • Showy and dramatic, alstroemerias are suitable for beginner gardeners and are sure to draw eyes when planted in a border. Modern cultivars of alstroemeria have an incredibly long flowering period, sending out flush after flush of brightly coloured flowers. They also – rather impressively – last some weeks in a vase.

Pitfalls • Alstroemerias loathe cold weather, heavy clay and shade, so if you have a damp outdoor space lacking in light, they probably won't fare well. Sometimes the stems can start to collapse under the weight of those cosmic blooms, so they may need staking or tying up with twine.

Did you know? • Despite its South American heritage, the plant is named after the Swedish naturalist who sent the seeds to Europe in the mid-1700s – Baron Claes Alströmer (1736–94).

Astrantia (*Astrantia major*)

✳	Flowers	June to September
✳	Foliage	Deciduous
✳	Height	1m
✳	Spread	60cm
✳	Preferred conditions	Dappled shade, partial shade, shade
✳	Origin	Europe
✳	Toxicity	Toxic to cats
✳	Also known as	Black hellebore, greater masterwort, Hattie's pincushion, melancholy gentleman

How to spot • Astrantia plants form clumps of lobed leaves at the base of the plant, with gossamer-like, wispy flowers held at the top of thin upright stalks. These flowers are distinctive because of the collar of petal-like bracts that encircle the pointillist central cluster of florets. Flowers traditionally appeared in pale pink tinged with green, but many pink and fuchsia varieties are now widely available.

Perks • Lace-like and delicate, astrantia flowers aren't just lauded for their ethereal beauty. They also offer nectar-rich sustenance for bees, butterflies and moths. Now regularly included in modern floral arrangements, the flowers have a long vase life and are also well suited to drying.

Author

Pitfalls • As in the case of so many things, it all comes down to a matter of taste – astrantia is beloved by many cottage gardeners, yet derided by those who prefer their flowers to arrive with a bit more oomph. (For what it's worth, in my shady garden, I'm firmly in the first group.) The plant can also be at risk of powdery mildew, which leaves unpleasant grey splotches on the foliage. Astrantia leaf miner larvae can also leave brown-grey patches on the leaves in early summer, but won't kill the plants.

Did you know? • The plant prefers shade because of its native habitat – the edges of alpine forests and meadows in Austria and Switzerland.

Border iris (*Iris germanica* and *Iris sibirica*)

Laura Ockel

Michele Dorsey Walfred

✳	**Flowers**	May to June
✳	**Foliage**	Deciduous
✳	**Height**	1.5m
✳	**Spread**	50cm
✳	**Preferred conditions**	Sun
✳	**Origin**	North America, Europe, Africa, Asia
✳	**Toxicity**	Toxic to humans, cats, dogs and horses
✳	**Also known as**	Siberian flag iris (*Iris sibirica*); common German flag, common iris, delicate iris, flag, flag iris, German iris, liberty iris, orrice root, orris root (*Iris germanica*)

How to spot • There are several hundred species of iris, but the most common you'll find in gardens and borders are – aptly – known as border irises. These are then separately categorised as either bearded irises (*Iris germanica*) or Siberian irises (*Iris sibirica*). Bearded irises are found in a wider colour range – from apricot to violet, blue, yellow, white or pink – while Siberian irises occur in purple, blue and yellow shades. Bearded irises have a short row of distinctive hairs in the inner petals, hence their name. Siberian irises have smaller flowers, but both have flattened, bright green leaves that grow in a bulb-like, clumping manner.

Perks • Irises are true perennials, which means they return year after year without losing their flower power or vigour, making them a trustworthy addition to a garden. Sometimes, during a particularly fine summer of sun, they will even reward you with a surprise second flush of flowering.

Pitfalls • They are pickier than some plants – Madame Bearded Iris *demands* full sun and will let you know if her home is too waterlogged, via an increased susceptibility to fungal and viral diseases and root rot. Siberian irises can get away with dappled shade. Also worth noting: ingestion of irises can cause severe stomach upset in humans.

Did you know? • Irises grow from rhizomes, a thick and fleshy root that sits horizontally beneath the soil.

Catmint (*Nepeta* spp.)

Author

✳	Flowers	June to August
✳	Foliage	Deciduous
✳	Height	1.5m
✳	Spread	60cm
✳	Preferred conditions	Sun
✳	Origin	Africa, Asia, Europe
✳	Toxicity	No reported toxicity
✳	Also known as	Catwort

How to spot • As the name suggests, you might be able to identify this plant if you notice a feline friend frequently paying it a visit – cats are attracted to its scent. If you're not party to that sight, look out for the soft greyish-green foliage that tends to flop onto the ground beneath the weight of the purple flowers. Blooms have a tubular shape and are popular with pollinators.

Perks • Catmint is an easy plant to grow in the correct conditions, not prone to pests or disease, and highly self-sufficient – the Jo March of the garden, if you will. The grey-tinged foliage combined with vivid purple flowers has earned catmint's place as a cottage garden favourite, and smaller varieties are particularly well suited to edging lawns, paths or borders.

Pitfalls • If you find catmint in a soggy spot, be aware that it may rot away and die – it much prefers dry, Mediterranean-like conditions. And if you're allergic or otherwise ambivalent to cats, perhaps you'd rather not harbour a plant with the potential to bring neighbourhood felines out in droves.

Did you know? • Catmint belongs to the mint family, like its close relatives lavender (p. 126) and thyme.

Chrysanthemum (*Chrysanthemum* spp.)

✳	Flowers	September to November
✳	Foliage	Deciduous
✳	Height	20cm
✳	Spread	1.5m
✳	Preferred conditions	Sun, dappled shade
✳	Origin	China
✳	Toxicity	Toxic to cats, dogs and horses
✳	Also known as	Chrysanths, garden mums, mums

Author

How to spot • Chrysanthemums vary widely in flower size, shape, colour, and hardiness. The foliage, however, grows in an alternating pattern, with scalloped leaves attached to the stem in a left–right fashion. The leaves have a slightly furry feel and are dark green in colour. Flowers can be large and showy, or held in small sprays – colours include yellow, orange, purple, pink, orange and more.

Perks • In sunny conditions, chrysanthemums will reward you with a beautiful display of autumn colour just as other summer-flowering plants are fading into insignificance. They also make long-lasting cut flowers. Today there are so many colours, shapes and sizes to choose from that we're really spoiled for choice. Early and hardy chrysanthemums are the easiest, most widely found and most reliable.

Pitfalls • You'll wait all summer for your chrysanthemums to flower and then sometimes, following cold wet summers, they'll put on a poor show. And it pays to identify what kind you have growing, as some tender varieties will not survive the winter and should be planted in pots that can be brought inside during the colder months.

Did you know? • Culturally and historically important in China – where it was first bred as a flowering herb – the chrysanthemum is the city flower of Beijing.

Coneflower (*Echinacea* spp.)

Author

✳	**Flowers**	July to October
✳	**Foliage**	Deciduous
✳	**Height**	1m
✳	**Spread**	50cm
✳	**Preferred conditions**	Sun
✳	**Origin**	North America
✳	**Toxicity**	No reported toxicity
✳	**Also known as**	Echinacea

How to spot • This popular perennial has lance-shaped, slightly hairy leaves and spiky flowers. The most widespread variety (*Echinacea purpurea*) has pinkish-purple blooms, but specimens with white, pale pink or orange flowers are also becoming a more frequent sight. The flower florets grow around a bristly central cone that points skywards.

Perks • Coneflowers offer late summer and autumn colour and are a firm favourite with bees and other pollinators. The plants look after themselves when planted in favourable conditions, rarely needing to be propped up with canes or watered. The dried seed heads can even be left on the plant for birds to enjoy.

Pitfalls • Echinacea can't stand a soggy bottom and is well-known for failing to survive cool, damp British winters. You'll also want to keep this plant out of the reach of curious children or pets, as the flowers are spiny to the touch.

Did you know? • Coneflowers are the main ingredient in herbal echinacea supplements sold to ward off the common cold.

Daffodil (*Narcissus* spp.)

✳	**Flowers**	January to May
✳	**Foliage**	Deciduous
✳	**Height**	50cm
✳	**Spread**	10cm
✳	**Preferred conditions**	Full sun, light shade
✳	**Origin**	northern Europe
✳	**Toxicity**	Toxic to humans, cats, dogs and horses

How to spot • Daffodils are one of our most recognisable spring flowers, extraordinarily common across the UK. In late winter or spring, the tips of the green leaves begin to appear above ground. Yellow or white flowers, most commonly trumpet-shaped, quickly bloom on long, single stems. There are now a wealth of varieties on offer, including double-petalled and bi-coloured varieties.

Perks • One of the jolliest sights of spring, daffodils are happy garden plants. They're simple to grow, needing virtually no tending to after planting, and make gloriously cheerful cut flowers. They are also one of the few bulbs that don't tickle the taste buds of mice and squirrels, so you can plant them without worrying they'll be dug up and devoured by garden rodents.

Annie Spratt

Pitfalls • After several years in the ground, daffodils can suffer from overcrowding (the bulbs having multiplied), leading to reduced or even absent flowering. The yellowed leaves, as is the case with most bulbs, need to be left to die back on the plant so nutrients can be fed back to the roots, which can look unappealing if not hidden by other later-flowering plants. They also don't offer much benefit to native wildlife, so are best planted alongside other nectar-rich flowers.

Did you know? • Large daffodil farms in Wales exist to breed a particular species of daffodil rich in a compound called galantamine, which is then used in pharmaceutical drugs that can slow the progress of Alzheimer's.

Delphinium (*Delphinium* spp.)

Rebecca Niver

✳	**Flowers**	June to September
✳	**Foliage**	Deciduous
✳	**Height**	1.5m
✳	**Spread**	1m
✳	**Preferred conditions**	Sun, dappled shade
✳	**Origin**	Northern Hemisphere, Africa
✳	**Toxicity**	Toxic to humans, cats, dogs and horses
✳	**Also known as**	Larkspur

How to spot • Look for delphiniums in late spring and early summer, when they are hard to miss – towering steeples of richly coloured flowers overshadow smaller plants in their midst. Their tall stature means they're often planted at the back of borders. The foliage sits in a clump at the base of the plant, and leaves are deeply lobed and shaped like a human hand. Flowers are most often a deep blue or purple, but pink, white and mauve varieties are also common these days.

Perks • Perennial delphiniums are a classic cottage garden plant, offering beauty, colour and height in the garden. The floral spires are so richly packed with flower heads, often of an intense blue unusual in nature, that they can be quite breathtaking. They also attract butterflies and pollinators, and make excellent cut flowers.

Pitfalls • Slugs and snails are well-known for decimating the fresh green shoots of delphiniums in the spring, sometimes to the extent that flowering is delayed or the plant does not recover. And the flowers sadly don't bloom continuously from June to September – after the first flush, cut back to the ground and you may get a second round of flowers in early autumn.

Did you know? • There are about 300 varieties of delphinium, and the flower has naturalised across North America.

Geum (*Geum* spp.)

Rachel Shillcock

✴ Flowers	April to October	
✴ Foliage	Semi-evergreen	
✴ Height	1m	
✴ Spread	60cm	
✴ Preferred conditions	Sun, dappled shade	
✴ Origin	Europe, Asia, North America, South America, South Africa, New Zealand	
✴ Toxicity	No reported toxicity	
✴ Also known as	Avens	

How to spot • Geum foliage grows in a clump at the base, and pompom-esque flowers are held on upright stalks – normally appearing in reds, oranges, peaches and yellows. Some can grow up to a metre in height, but most average about 60cm tall by 60cm wide. The leaves are rounded at their edges and grow in a rosette formation.

Perks • Geums are easy to grow and faithfully reliable – even those common garden marauders, slugs and deer, aren't overly fond of nibbling on them. Why remains a mystery given that geum's merry appearance is so bright and enticing they wouldn't look amiss on the shelf of an old-fashioned sweet shop. Their diminutive stature makes them ideal for the front of a border or raised bed.

Pitfalls • Some varieties of geum only flower for a month or two in the spring, while others offer a metered flow of blooms throughout the summer season. Only close observation and time will tell which you have if you are unsure of the variety you're inspecting. After a few years in the same spot, geums can become crowded and will need to be divided to ensure the plant continues to flower well.

Did you know? • Geum 'Totally Tangerine' – a long-flowering, citrus-coloured cultivar – won Plant of the Year at the Chelsea Flower Show in 2010.

Globe thistle (*Echinops ritro*)

✴ Flowers	July to August
✴ Foliage	Deciduous
✴ Height	1m
✴ Spread	50cm
✴ Preferred conditions	Sun, dappled shade
✴ Origin	Europe, Asia
✴ Toxicity	No reported toxicity
✴ Also known as	Blue hedgehog, globe flower

Author   *Author*

How to spot • There are several different types of globe thistles grown in gardens and sold in garden centres, varying in height and size, but *Echinops ritro* is probably the most widespread. However, all kinds have spherical, purple-blue flower heads and webbed foliage that forms in clumps at the base of the plant. The stems are sturdy and sit upright, with the clusters of bauble-like flowers at the very tip.

Perks • Like the aesthetically similar sea holly (p. 89), the globe thistle's striking colour and unusual foliage means it packs a punch in a border. In high summer, when the globe thistle is in full bloom, the plants will appear to emit a constant, steady hum. No, they haven't learned to sing – it's the sound of a ceaseless stream of visiting bees. If you leave the seed heads to dry on the plant, small songbirds will also visit the plant in autumn to feast on the seeds.

Pitfalls • Compared to some other perennials, the globe thistle has a relatively short flowering period – just two months at the height of summer. Deadheading the flowers, however, may encourage a second round of blooms.

Did you know? • The plant's Latin name derives from the Greek 'echinos', meaning hedgehog, a nod to the globe thistle's spiny appearance.

Hardy geranium (*Geranium* spp.)

Author

✳	**Flowers**	May to October
✳	**Foliage**	Deciduous
✳	**Height**	50cm
✳	**Spread**	70cm
✳	**Preferred conditions**	Dappled shade, partial shade
✳	**Origin**	Southern Africa, although the UK has some native varieties
✳	**Toxicity**	No reported toxicity
✳	**Also known as**	Cranesbill, true geraniums

How to spot • Hardy geraniums are long-standing favourites in gardens across the UK, prized for their long flowering period and ability to act as aesthetically pleasing ground cover. The hand-shaped leaves may be slightly or extremely furred, and flowers come in colours ranging from white to purple to pink.

Author

Perks • These garden favourites occupy their position for good reason. They are easy to grow and often produce several flushes of flowers in a single season, especially if cut right back to the base after the initial bloom. Purple-flowered Geranium 'Rozanne' is a particularly luminescent cultivar, and one of my favourites. It produces an abundance of electric blue-purple flowers from early summer until the first frosts.

Pitfalls • The main drawback of hardy geraniums is that they can outgrow their space and shade out other plants, in which case division and cutting back can become necessary. Sometimes they are targeted by a pest called geranium sawfly, which can shred the leaves and leave unsightly damage – but it is generally not damaging to the roots, so the plant will survive.

Did you know? • Talk about a teacher's pet – research estimates that around 40 million geraniums are planted in the UK every single year.[1]

---

1. Source: Pelargonium for Europe, www.pelargoniumforeurope.com/en

Hellebores (*Helleborus* spp.)

Author

✳	**Flowers**	December to March
✳	**Foliage**	Evergreen
✳	**Height**	60cm
✳	**Spread**	60cm
✳	**Preferred conditions**	Light shade
✳	**Origin**	Middle East
✳	**Toxicity**	Toxic to humans, cats, dogs and horses
✳	**Also known as**	Christmas rose, Lenten rose, winter rose

How to spot • Look for hellebores in light shade, often thriving at the base of trees. The dark green, shiny foliage is usually evergreen and often sports attractive marbled markings. The leaves are divided into distinct leaflets. From late winter to early spring, nodding, cup-shaped flowers form, attracting early pollinating insects. Their bright white or pink hue often appears to glow against the dark winter soil.

Perks • These are a rare gem when it comes to herbaceous perennial flowers in this country, blooming as they do in winter or early spring. And the fact that they come into flower when little else is around to offer floral sustenance makes them even more of a treasure. Add to that their striking greenery, and shade-tolerant demeanour, and you've got a real winner.

WHAT IS THAT PLANT?

Valleybrook Gardens

Pitfalls • That arresting foliage comes with a cost – it's vulnerable to various fungal and viral diseases, like the very common hellebore leaf spot. This sees dark splotches appear on the leaves. Affected leaves should be removed and destroyed, rather than composted, as soon as you notice them.

Did you know? • The plants are also known as Christmas roses, referring to their flowering season, although they're actually in the buttercup family.

Heuchera (*Heuchera* spp.)

Valleybrook Gardens

Valleybrook Gardens   *Valleybrook Gardens*

✳	**Flowers**	May to August
✳	**Foliage**	Evergreen
✳	**Height**	50cm
✳	**Spread**	50cm
✳	**Preferred conditions**	Partial shade, shade
✳	**Origin**	North America
✳	**Toxicity**	No reported toxicity
✳	**Also known as**	Alumroot, coral bells

How to spot • Look for happy heucheras in shady borders, beneath trees or in woodland conditions. The plant has shallow, woody roots and radiant foliage that comes in a range of bright and neon colours, as well as green, often with visible dark or brightly coloured veins on top. The sides of the leaves are frilled, like the edges of a lace doily. Lightweight spikes topped with delicate flowers rise like lit candles from the base of the plant in late spring and early summer, although in milder areas you may see flowers beginning to bloom as early as March.

Perks • In the past heucheras were better known for their spikes of fluorescent blooms, but in recent years, plant breeders have gone to town on the foliage – cultivating hundreds of different varieties, from those with lime green leaves to fire orange and burgundy alongside an array of interesting leaf markings. They're fully hardy across the UK and very reliable and easy to care for. I especially like the way the slender flowers sway in the early June breeze.

Pitfalls • After a few years, heuchera tend to need dividing to keep them going – but once you know how, that shouldn't be a problem. They can also fall victim to one of the very few pests that affect them – vine weevils can chew on the leaves overnight, leaving unsightly notches at the edges of the foliage. Left to feast, they will move onto the roots, eventually killing the plant.

Did you know? • Heuchera is named after the German botanist Johann H. von Heucher (1677–1747).

Hosta (*Hosta* spp.)

John Matychuk

✴ **Flowers**	July to October
✴ **Foliage**	Deciduous
✴ **Height**	50cm
✴ **Spread**	1m
✴ **Preferred conditions**	Shade
✴ **Origin**	Asia
✴ **Toxicity**	Toxic to cats, dogs and horses
✴ **Also known as**	Funkia, plantain lily

Mary Hammel

How to spot • Identifying hostas by their foliage is probably your best bet – these shade-loving plants are prized for their satin-like foliage that grows in domed mounds. If you stroke the edge of the leaves, you will feel smooth edges and prominent veins running along the underside of each leaf. Foliage is green, but can have pale green, white or yellow stripes or edges. Tubular flowers, which bloom in midsummer, are usually blue, white, pink or lilac and are held aloft on narrow stems.

Perks • Hostas' interesting leaves can bring much-needed light to shady corners of a garden. They also live, and flower well, for many years, while being low maintenance and easy to establish. Different varieties flower at different points in the summer, too, so if you have inherited a broad selection – or choose to plant a mixture – you can enjoy hosta blooms all summer long.

Pitfalls • Hosta leaves are loved by slugs and snails almost as much as they are by the gardening establishment. Deer and rabbits also love taking a bite out of their apparently tasty foliage.

Did you know? • Hostas are another example of an Asian plant being named after a European botanist – in this case, Austrian botanist Nicholas Thomas Host (1761–1834).

Japanese anemone (*Anemone japonica*)

Author

✳	**Flowers**	August to October
✳	**Foliage**	Deciduous
✳	**Height**	1.2m
✳	**Spread**	60cm
✳	**Preferred conditions**	Sun, partial shade
✳	**Origin**	China
✳	**Toxicity**	No reported toxicity
✳	**Also known as**	Chinese anemone, thimbleweed, windflower

How to spot • When in flower, delicate white or pink flowers with yellow centres appear to float at the top of tall, wiry stems, often dancing in the breeze. The leaves are trifoliate, meaning divided into three leaflets. The foliage is deeply defined, and glossy dark green in colour – turn over a leaf and you'll find a dull, pale underside.

Perks • Dainty flowers, late summer colour in shades of white and pink, lofty in height but feathery enough to retain a view through their stems: Japanese anemones have many plus points. They are particularly well suited to growing in large drifts – if you're lucky enough to have the space – where their bobbing heads will sway in the breeze, lending them their common name 'windflowers'.

Pitfalls • Arm yourself with the knowledge that this plant spreads by underground stems and has been known to go rogue when it finds a spot it likes. The white variety *Anemone x hybrida* is more easily contained. As Japanese anemones only flower in the autumn, the foliage can look dull for much of the year, and takes up quite a lot of space.

Did you know? • Despite what their name would have you expect, Japanese anemones in fact originated in China. Their common name comes from the fact that they have been cultivated and naturalised in Japan for centuries – this was where European colonists first discovered the plant.

Lamb's ear (*Stachys byzantina*)

Author

✳ **Flowers**	June to July
✳ **Foliage**	Evergreen
✳ **Height**	50cm
✳ **Spread**	1m
✳ **Preferred conditions**	Sun, dappled shade
✳ **Origin**	the Middle East
✳ **Toxicity**	No reported toxicity
✳ **Also known as**	Bear's ear, bunnie ears, mouse ear, rabbit ear, oat's ear, lamb's tongue, lamb's wood, woolly hedgenettle

How to spot • Reach out to touch the unusually coloured foliage of *Stachys byzantina* and you'll find it downy to the touch – hence the common names referencing furry creatures. In June and July, pale pinkish-purple flowers grow in a tiered fashion on spires that can rise up to half a metre above the silver leaves. The foliage spreads, carpet-like, across the surrounding earth, proving particularly sprawling in nutritious soil.

Perks • Silver foliage is having a moment and lamb's ear certainly fulfils that brief. Even if you're not a fan, one of Britain's largest solitary bees – the wool carder bee – is; these pollinators scrape hair from the woolly leaves to use for nest-building.

Pitfalls • Some see the flowers as dull and inconspicuous, partially hidden as they are among the stems. They are also liable to spread widely in rich earth, so you may eventually find pulling up their plentiful offspring more trouble than they're worth.

Did you know? • With lamb's ear, you can gain new plants by division – cut into existing clumps of foliage in autumn or winter with a sharp spade and replant some of the new offcuts elsewhere.

Lupin (*Lupinus* spp.)

✳ **Flowers**	May to June, August
✳ **Foliage**	Deciduous
✳ **Height**	1.2m
✳ **Spread**	50cm
✳ **Preferred conditions**	Full sun, dappled shade
✳ **Origin**	the Mediterranean
✳ **Toxicity**	Toxic to humans, cats, dogs and horses
✳ **Also known as**	Lupine

How to spot • Lupins are distinctive plants, both in foliage and flower. The unusual leaves are grey–green and shaped like stars. The flowers appear in whorls on upright spires and have been developed in a wide range of colours, from muted pastels to bright scarlets and yellows. Identification may also be helped by checking for pests: aphids love to feast on the leaves, as do slugs and snails, so you may notice bites taken out of the foliage.

Perks • Lupins offer eye-catching spring colour and interesting greenery to boot. The stellate leaves are singular in shape, and the florets at their prime so bright and dazzling that they almost seem to glow.

Aleksandra Sapozhnikova

Pitfalls • Keep away from areas where curious children and pets might wander – they can prove poisonous if ingested. Restrict access by slugs too (easier said than done) as they will gladly munch young plants away to nothing. The leaves are also prone to powdery mildew, leaving unpleasant grey speckles on the foliage.

Did you know? • Lupini beans, traditionally consumed as a pickled snack in Italy, are the seeds of the lupin plant and rich in protein.

Joshua Tree National Park

Michaelmas daisy (*Aster* spp.)

Author

✳	**Flowers**	July to October
✳	**Foliage**	Deciduous
✳	**Height**	1m
✳	**Spread**	50cm
✳	**Preferred conditions**	Light shade
✳	**Origin**	Europe, Asia
✳	**Toxicity**	No reported toxicity
✳	**Also known as**	Asters, autumn asters, symphyotrichum

How to spot • The best time to spot Michaelmas daisies is in the early autumn, when plants produce a profusion of daisy-like blooms. The flowers are most often lilac, with yellow centres, but some varieties are pink, white or a deeper purple. Foliage and stems can vary in shape or size.

Perks • Many gardeners appreciate Michaelmas daisies for their striking display of autumn colour, when many summer plants have ceased blooming. Bees and butterflies are fans of the purple flowers, too. The plants have an airy profile, so they can be used to good effect in a flower bed or mixed border, allowing light and air to flow through them and not disrupting the view to plants behind them.

Pitfalls • Michaelmas daisies are sometimes viewed as weeds – left to their own accord, they will self-seed quite happily, multiplying their number quite dramatically. In one churchyard in Oxford I walk through often they've been allowed to do just that, at the expense of other plants, and are beginning to look slightly forlorn. However, keeping an eye on them should rein in these tendencies.

Did you know? • The name Michaelmas daisy was chosen because the flowers bloom in time for Michaelmas, a Christian festival that celebrates the Archangel Michael.

Penstemon (*Penstemon* spp.)

✳	**Flowers**	June to October
✳	**Foliage**	Semi-evergreen
✳	**Height**	1m
✳	**Spread**	60cm
✳	**Preferred conditions**	Sun
✳	**Origin**	North America, Asia
✳	**Toxicity**	No reported toxicity
✳	**Also known as**	Beardtongue

Author

How to spot • Penstemon are bushy plants once they have been left to establish for a few years, although the evergreen leaves themselves are narrow and delicate. The stems can be dark red or green, with leaves growing on either side of each flowering stalk. Some varieties are low growing, while others can reach a metre in height after several years. The flowers have a very pronounced funnel shape, like foxgloves (p. 74), and visiting bees can often be seen crawling into them. Flowers can be a variety of colours, from white to pink to purple to red, and some varieties have contrasting white throats.

Perks • Bees love the tubular flowers as much as I do. Bonus points, too, for novice gardeners –

penstemon are reliable flowerers and simple to care for, except in areas that have very cold winters. They bloom for a long season – in my area still pushing out flowers well into October or milder Novembers – and are very accepting of long periods without rain, an attribute that is becoming increasingly advantageous in British summers.

Pitfalls • For all their appealing floral attributes, penstemon foliage is rather inconspicuous – although it does have its semi-evergreen status to fall back on. The plants can also become overly woody as the years pass and are best kept in check by pruning right back to the ground after the final spring frosts.

Did you know? • The colloquial name 'beardtongue' – frequently used in America – originates from varieties that have flowers with hairy throats.

Peony (*Paeonia* spp.)

Marta Filipczyk

✳	**Flowers**	May to June
✳	**Foliage**	Deciduous
✳	**Height**	1m
✳	**Spread**	1m
✳	**Preferred conditions**	Sun
✳	**Origin**	Asia
✳	**Toxicity**	Toxic to cats, dogs and horses

How to spot • Peonies can thrive for decades with little fuss so if you see a plant that returns every spring, with thick, waxy, well-defined leaves and large, blowsy, cupped flowers in late spring in shades ranging from white to pale pink to ruby red you could be looking at a peony. Herbaceous peonies die back fully in autumn before emerging as bright red shoots in early spring, so you won't find these in your garden in the autumn or winter.

Perks • As long as the crowns of peonies are baked by the sun in early spring, they should bloom beautifully, rewarding you with a voluptuous display of flowers. These are so vivid and large that it can be hard to drag your eyes away from them! They are extraordinarily popular cut flowers these days, and expensive too, so having your own supply to pick from is a treat.

Pitfalls • Peonies are creatures of habit – homebodies so to speak – and they particularly dislike being uprooted and moved. It can take years for a plant to recover from such an upheaval, during which time it will generally refuse to flower. And while the flowers are cult classics for good reason, their flowering period is incredibly short – mere weeks. Some would say this makes them all the more special, while others think they're not worth the space they take up for that reason.

Did you know? • Peony plants are one of the longest-lived perennials, with some still producing flowers after 100 years.

Perennial phlox (*Phlox paniculata*)

Author

✳ Flowers	June to September	
✳ Foliage	Deciduous	
✳ Height	1m	
✳ Spread	1m	
✳ Preferred conditions	Sun, dappled shade, partial shade	
✳ Origin	North America	
✳ Toxicity	No reported toxicity	
✳ Also known as	Border phlox, garden phlox, summer phlox, tall phlox	

How to spot • Perennial phlox is best identified in summer, when its perfumed flowers are in full bloom. The flowers come in a variety of shades, including blue, purple, pink, red and white. They are held in dense clusters, known as panicles, at the top of the stems.

Perks • Sweet scented and long flowering, border phlox is also a favourite of nectar-seeking bees and butterflies. The plants last for many years, continuing to flower well, and the cheerful blooms make superb cut flowers. And phlox is suited to a variety of aspects – minding neither sun nor partial shade. Grow close to your back door to make the most of its scent.

Pitfalls • In hot and humid conditions, phlox foliage may suffer from powdery mildew, while drought can cause the leaves to wilt.

Did you know? • Another type of phlox – the annual kind that lives for only one season – can be grown from seed or picked up relatively cheaply from garden centres as bedding plants. They're smaller in stature and work well in pots.

Red hot poker (*Kniphofia* spp.)

✳ Flowers	March to November
✳ Foliage	Evergreen
✳ Height	2.1m
✳ Spread	1m
✳ Preferred conditions	Sun
✳ Origin	Africa
✳ Toxicity	No reported toxicity
✳ Also known as	Torch lily

Author   *Eleanor Burfitt*

How to spot • There are few plants quite like red hot pokers – their intensely coloured flowers look like blazing torches (hence the nickname torch lily). They wouldn't look amiss on stage at a circus! *Kniphofia* leaves are grass-like, forming in clumps at the base of the plant. The most common cultivar has flowers shaded orange, red and yellow – with the flowers progressively turning pale yellow from the bottom of the petals up, developing the appearance of a lit match. Today, flowers are also seen in pinks, browns and a wider variety of sunset tones.

Perks • It's hard to think of a more dramatic and architecturally striking plant than the red hot poker. And better yet, different varieties flower at different points of the summer, so a careful curation of varieties can guarantee flowering from March to November. They love to bathe in bright, hot sun so are perfect for a south-facing dry garden.

Pitfalls • Red hot pokers don't like wet winters, so may not survive the colder months in areas that get a lot of rainfall. Hungry slugs and snails can overwinter among the foliage, ready to feast on fresh new growth in the spring. And they need ample space to spread their roots and leaves, with some varieties spreading up to a metre wide.

Did you know? • Hailing from sunny South Africa, gardeners at London's Kew Gardens in the 1840s were surprised when a few specimens of *Kniphofia* survived a cold winter outside – and so began their ascent to popularity in Britain.

Rose campion (*Lychnis coronaria*)

Nikita Turkovich

✳	**Flowers**	June to August
✳	**Foliage**	Deciduous
✳	**Height**	1m
✳	**Spread**	50cm
✳	**Preferred conditions**	Sun
✳	**Origin**	Europe, Asia
✳	**Toxicity**	No reported toxicity
✳	**Also known as**	Bloody campion, Bridget-in-her-bravery, campion, corn rose, crown of the field, dusty miller, garland flower, pink mullein, red bird's eye, rose cockle

How to spot • The unusual-coloured foliage of rose campion makes it easy to identify, as one of just a few outliers among perennials in this part of the world. The leaves are a pale grey–green with a soft, felted texture when touched. In the summer, masses of simple magenta flowers emerge at the very tip of each stem, attracting bees and butterflies.

Perks • This romantic, old-fashioned plant is a cottage garden favourite for good reason, with its attractive long-lasting flowers and eye-catching foliage. In its preferred conditions of full sun and dry soil, it will merrily self-seed, gifting you extra plants with no effort or investment needed on your part.

Pitfalls • While rose campion isn't vulnerable to any significant pests or diseases, overwatering – or a very rainy season – will cause its roots to rot, eventually leading to plant death. Its self-seeding tendencies are loved by some, loathed by others.

Did you know? • The term 'coronaria' in the plant's Latin botanical name means 'garland', as rose campion was thought to have been used to make wreaths for victorious athletes.

Scabious (*Scabiosa* spp.)

Author

✴ **Flowers**	June to August
✴ **Foliage**	Deciduous or semi-evergreen
✴ **Height**	1m
✴ **Spread**	1m
✴ **Preferred conditions**	Sun
✴ **Origin**	Europe, Asia, Africa
✴ **Toxicity**	No reported toxicity
✴ **Also known as**	Garden scabious, pincushion flower

How to spot • The name pincushion flower provides clues to successful identification of scabious: look for button-like, ruffled flowers, often with a domed appearance that appears studded as though by dressmakers' pins. Depending on the variety, flowers are commonly white, pink, purple or deep red. *Scabiosa caucasica* is a classic variety, with lilac blue flowers. The frilly foliage is usually grey–green in colour and congregates at the base of the plant, with the flowers held on slender, wiry stems.

Perks • Scabious is particularly prized by butterflies, with one popular variety named Butterfly Blue. They are also a good option for cut flowers. And in milder areas, some types will continue to flower well into the winter months.

Pitfalls • The plant will fail to flower or thrive in shady spots. And it's a shame about the name – such a pretty blossom deserves something a bit more elegant, don't you think?

Did you know? • The name does, however reveal something of the plant's background – in the past, its antipruritic tendencies were prized for relieving the itching that accompanies the disease scabies.

Sedum (*Hylotelephium spectabile*)

Author

Valleybrook Gardens

✳	**Flowers**	August to October
✳	**Foliage**	Deciduous
✳	**Height**	50cm
✳	**Spread**	50cm
✳	**Preferred conditions**	Sun
✳	**Origin**	Northern Hemisphere and mountains in the tropics
✳	**Toxicity**	No reported toxicity
✳	**Also known as**	Stonecrop

How to spot • The leaves of sedum plants may look familiar to you if you're an avid houseplant custodian – they're a type of succulent perennial so their foliage has the same fleshy look as the indoor plants that have become fashionable to raise inside in recent years. In late summer and into autumn, flat heads of deep pink flowers attract bees and butterflies.

Perks • Sedum is easy to grow, requiring little special care, and provides a wonderful burst of autumn colour on a plot. They're so used to drought conditions, too, that they make an excellent choice for green roofs or gravel gardens. And the bees are big fans as well.

Pitfalls • Sedums are partial to dry, sandy soils, so you may find they flower poorly in nutritious soils and on heavy clay. Fertilising will usually make little difference in this instance, so it's best to uproot to a place with less abundant earth.

Did you know? • Taking cuttings from sedum is simple and means you can pass on new plants to others. Snip a 5cm shoot off the plant, opting for a stem without a bud, remove the lower leaves and place in a glass of water, where it will grow roots. Once a visible section of root has formed, repot into a small container to grow on.

Snowdrop (*Galanthus* spp.)

Author

✳	**Flowers**	January to March
✳	**Foliage**	Deciduous
✳	**Height**	20cm
✳	**Spread**	50cm
✳	**Preferred conditions**	Partial shade
✳	**Origin**	Europe, the Middle East
✳	**Toxicity**	Toxic to humans, cats, dogs and horses
✳	**Also known as**	Candlemas bells, Candlemas lily, common bells, death's flower, dewdrops, drooping bell, February fair-maids, little sister of the snows

How to spot • Strap-shaped, narrow green leaves surround stalks that rise no more than 20cm above the ground – and most varieties are smaller than this still. You're most likely to identify them in dappled shade; they rarely thrive in full sun. The bell-shaped white flowers have three inner petals and three external petals, with delicate green markings. Different varieties can vary in size and height. Their leaves echo those of other spring bulbs but generally appear much earlier in the calendar year than later-flowering specimens.

Perks • When scant else is in flower, the nodding milk-white heads of snowdrops are a welcome sight. Many see them as the first sign that spring is on its way.

Pitfalls • Blink and you'll miss them! If you're more used to spending time on the sofa in midwinter (and I don't blame you), then the arrival of snowdrops might pass you by entirely.

Did you know? • Johann Strauss II composed his waltz *Schneeglöckchen* (Snowdrops) op. 143 in honour of the flower.

Spring crocus (*Crocus* spp.)

Eleanor Burfitt

✳ Flowers	February to March
✳ Foliage	Deciduous
✳ Height	10cm
✳ Spread	10cm
✳ Preferred conditions	Sun
✳ Origin	the Mediterranean, Asia
✳ Toxicity	Toxic to cats, dogs and horses
✳ Also known as	Spring-flowering crocus

How to spot • Crocuses are familiar to many, as one of the first hopeful signs of spring. Purple, yellow, white, or lilac, the small, bowl-shaped flowers are found in woodland, lawns and gardens. The leaves are grass-like, and striped green and white, but quickly obscured by the flowers, which have bright yellow centres.

Perks • As one of the first spring (or late winter) flowers, crocuses are a cheerful harbinger of warmer days. After several years, the plants often spread to form dense carpets of flowers – a stunning sight. They're cheap to buy, simple to grow and very quick to establish, so a good choice for beginners.

Pitfalls • The biggest blight on crocuses is how tasty they are – at least where squirrels and mice are concerned. Squirrels are well-known for digging up the bulbs to eat before they have flowered. They are also susceptible to incurable viral diseases that can impair or prevent flowering.

Did you know? • There's also an autumn-flowering crocus, known as meadow saffron.

Tulip (*Tulipa* spp.)

✳ Flowers	April to May
✳ Foliage	Deciduous
✳ Height	70cm
✳ Spread	25cm
✳ Preferred conditions	Full sun, dappled shade
✳ Origin	Asia
✳ Toxicity	Toxic to humans, cats, dogs and horses

Author   *Yoksel Zok*

How to spot • These incredibly common spring bulbs are difficult to avoid in April and May in Britain – and would you want to? Few will fail to be moved by the sight of their colourful heads bobbing in a spring breeze after a long, cold winter. The leaves are long and oval, upright at first, but often bending once the plant is in flower. Blooms come in all manner of colours these days, from muted whites and pinks to jewel-like brights. As the flowers go over, petals will fall to the ground, leaving the stamen and pistil bare.

Perks • Tulips are quintessential spring flowers, and in my view one can never have too many. Today there are so many colours, shapes and sizes to choose from – whether frilly parrot tulips in pastel hues or more simple single tulips in jewel-like shades. They're so widely popular and relatively inexpensive that you're more likely than not to find them popping up in your outdoor space or local park. And gardener or not, you most likely already know they are dependable cut flowers, having seen cheerful bunches sold in supermarkets as early as January.

Pitfalls • Over several years of repeat flowering, tulips will become smaller and smaller, so you may wish to dig up the bulbs once this occurs. Some dislike the way the petals fall off the plant as the flower dies back, but I enjoy the way they exit in a blaze of glorious decay, rather than softly slipping away.

Did you know? • Most will be aware of the connection between the Netherlands and tulips. But that link became a little too close for comfort when the Dutch resorted to eating tulip bulbs in the great famine of 1944–45.

Self-seeders & spreaders

Self-seeding and spreading plants can be a great friend to gardeners. These eager 'volunteer' plants sow themselves into nooks and crannies with little to no human input required. By the same metric, self-seeders and spreaders can also be seen as a bit of a nuisance, creating extra work for gardeners when they need evicting from places they have spread to without invitation, or have taken over bare soil relatively quickly.

Such plants tend to be annuals (growing, flowering, and setting seed in the space of one year) or biennials (which grow, flower, and set seed in two years). But some perennials are vigorous self-seeders too (looking at you, lady's mantle! - see p. 78). They scatter their seed generously over the surrounding soil during their lifetime to ensure the survival of their genes. Over time, and often in the space of just a few months, these seeds grow into new plants, making a home in nearby borders, between cracks in the patio or in small gaps in garden walls.

By their very nature, self-seeders can be tricky to identify. It is not uncommon to see them popping up a fair distance from their parent plant, sneaking under neighbouring fences or deposited onto soil by animals or the wind. Despite this, it's well worth trying to verify the identity of potential self-sowers in your garden. The ability to tell them apart from unwanted weeds means you can make sure you're not accidentally nurturing something that will take over at the expense of all other plants. Successful identification also means you can give plants the correct care and if you aren't keen on where self-sown seeds have decided to germinate, you can transplant them to somewhere more suitable or pass them on to friends.

In spring, keep an eye out for seedlings in your borders that look similar to annual or biennial plants you grew last year. If it's your first year in a new garden, it's worth letting whatever pops up in springtime grow a little larger than you might otherwise to give you a better shot at identification. Countless flower species will self-seed if given the opportunity, but some varieties are well-known for their bountiful breeding. And, of course, many plants classed as weeds and wildflowers are self-seeders by nature (see p. 149). The following chapter lists some of the most prolific self-seeders found in British borders, pavements and patios.

Allium (*Allium* spp.)

Author

Richard Loader

★ Flowers	April to June
★ Foliage	Deciduous
★ Height	1m
★ Spread	50cm
★ Preferred conditions	Sun, dappled shade
★ Origin	Northern Hemisphere
★ Toxicity	Toxic to cats, dogs and horses

How to spot • Alliums grow on tall, leafless, single stems, with long and slender foliage either side, just like fellow bulbs tulips and daffodils. Before their buds open, alliums might be mistaken for other flowering bulbs, or even poppy heads, but once they open, their purple flowers and striking seed heads are hard to miss. White, green and pink cultivars are also available.

Perks • Offering stunning colour in spring, alliums are more reliable than tulips and beloved by bees. They don't take up much space and provide lasting interest, as their flowers turn to golden seed heads in midsummer. And the fact they multiply year on year only adds to their charm, in this author's opinion!

Pitfalls • Little to note here, except that the foliage can begin to look slightly unkempt as the flowers appear and go over. However, unlike other bulbs, this can be safely removed without damaging the plant.

Did you know? • Ornamental alliums such as those described above should not be eaten, but edible alliums – garlic, onions, leeks and chives – do belong to the same plant family.

Aquilegia (*Aquilegia* spp.)

★ Flowers	May to June
★ Foliage	Deciduous
★ Height	1m
★ Spread	50cm
★ Preferred conditions	Sun, partial shade
★ Origin	Europe, Asia
★ Toxicity	Toxic to humans, cats, dogs and horses
★ Also known as	American bluebells, American snapdragon, culverwort, dove plant, God's breath, granny's bonnets, lady's shoes, lion's herb, naked woman's foot, pigeon flower, sow wort

Mats Hagwall

How to spot • Aquilegias are sometimes called granny's bonnets, and you can see why: the small flowers sit like old-fashioned hats at the top of elegant, long, narrow stems. Some newer cultivars have double layers of petals, but the common columbine (*Aquilegia vulgaris*) native to British woodlands has a single layer of blue petals on each flower. Varieties are available in a range of flower colours, including pink, magenta, blue, yellow, or white. Some flowers are two-toned, others one colour. The plant's foliage is distinctive, too: attractive green leaves, three per stem, flaunt scalloped edges (like buttercups, in the same family). They're found in damp woodlands, fens and in gardens.

Perks • If you're lucky enough to be the recipient of a self-seeded aquilegia or five, enjoy their flowering period in May and June – a time in the UK growing season when tulips and daffodils are going over, and gardens can suffer from a dearth of colour. Aquilegias work particularly well in gardens with a wild look, due to their free and easy self-seeding.

Patrick Alexander

Pitfalls • Have one aquilegia, have many – you'll find them popping up everywhere! For some, this will be less than desirable. The leaves are also commonly affected by powdery mildew, but will usually regrow quickly – and healthily – if chopped back to the base.

Did you know? • Aquilegias are sometimes called dove plants because the flowers are said to resemble a circle of five doves.

Bear's breeches (*Acanthus mollis*)

Laura Ockel

✳	**Flowers**	July to August
✳	**Foliage**	Deciduous
✳	**Height**	1.5m
✳	**Spread**	1.5m
✳	**Preferred conditions**	Sun, partial shade
✳	**Origin**	Europe, Africa, Asia
✳	**Toxicity**	No reported toxicity
✳	**Also known as**	Acanthus, brank ursine

How to spot • Bear's breeches grow at such scale that it's hard to miss them. Once the plant has settled in, huge, serrated leaves with a dull, matt sheen crowd the bottom of the plant. In midsummer, sturdy columns of flowers rise to heights of 1.5m. The creamy blooms have an upper and lower lip, with the latter gradually fading to a deep purple as the season progresses.

Perks • If you want to make a statement, then bear's breeches will certainly do so. Imposing and statuesque, the flower spikes offer many of the benefits of lupins, yet are less vulnerable to slug attacks. The flowers work well in dried arrangements, too.

Pitfalls • Those colossal leaves have soft-spiny edges, so it's best to wear gloves when handling and keep inquisitive children beyond arm's reach. And this probably isn't the best pick for small places. I have also heard bear's breeches described as a melancholy plant, with its funereal colouring and imposing leaves – all a matter of taste in the end.

Did you know? • Another *Acanthus* – *Acanthus spinosus* – is very similar but prefers to grow in shady spots. It has glossier leaves with prickly edges.

Bluebell (*Hyacinthoides non-scripta*)

Mark Fairhurst

✳ Flowers	April to May
✳ Foliage	Deciduous
✳ Height	50cm
✳ Spread	1m
✳ Preferred conditions	Sun, partial shade
✳ Origin	Europe
✳ Toxicity	Toxic to humans, cats, dogs and horses
✳ Also known as	Fairy flower, wood bell

How to spot • Many will be familiar with the stunning carpets of bluebells that sweep through Britain's woodlands each spring. And these petite flowers also pop up frequently in gardens and on street corners. The small plant has strap-shaped green leaves and drooping, blue bell-shaped flowers. The English bluebell has white, creamy pollen and a soft, subtle scent.

Perks • Few can fail to be cheered by the sight of the bluebell's dainty bobbing heads – there's a reason why bluebell woods draw crowds. In the right conditions (slightly shady, damp soil) they will spread naturally by both seed and bulb division and bring springtime joy to your plot.

Author

Pitfalls • Bluebells can spread quickly, outcompeting weaker garden plants. To limit their onward march, you can remove the flower heads after the flowers go over and dig up any bulbs you don't want to keep.

Did you know? • In the UK, English bluebells are protected by law, and it is illegal to dig them up in the wild. This country's native variety is at risk from the Spanish bluebell (*Hyacinthoides hispanica*). Now common in gardens across the UK, the Spanish variety and its hybrid offspring have paler flowers and are unscented. While a pretty flower in its own right, it is much more rapacious than the English type and some experts are worried it will ultimately lead to the extinction of *Hyacinthoides non-scripta*.

Borage (*Borago officinalis*)

✳	**Flowers**	June to October
✳	**Foliage**	Deciduous
✳	**Height**	90cm
✳	**Spread**	90cm
✳	**Preferred conditions**	Sun, partial shade
✳	**Origin**	the Mediterranean
✳	**Toxicity**	Toxic to cats, dogs and horses
✳	**Also known as**	Cool tankard, star flower, tailwort

Author

How to spot • This bee-friendly, edible plant has blue, star-shaped blossoms with a violet tinge and stems with a rough, hairy feel and appearance. You'll find it in full sun buzzing with bees and butterflies.

Perks • If it's popped up on your veg patch or allotment, it's worth keeping as it will attract pollinators to your plot, particularly honey and bumblebees – both adore its rich nectar. The star-shaped flowers do make a colourful addition to salads and cocktails. The leaves have a cucumber-like taste, making them a useful salad crop.

Pitfalls • In an ornamental border, borage can begin to look slightly straggly as the season progresses. If you have sensitive skin, it's advisable to wear gloves when pruning or weeding borage as its hairy leaves can cause surface irritation.

Did you know? • The ancient Greeks and Romans, including Pliny the Elder (AD 23/24-79) believe borage bestowed courage on those who consumed it. For that reason it was allegedly given to soldiers to eat before heading into battle.

California poppy (*Eschscholzia californica*)

Author

✳	**Flowers**	June to October
✳	**Foliage**	Deciduous
✳	**Height**	50cm
✳	**Spread**	50cm
✳	**Preferred conditions**	Sun
✳	**Origin**	North America
✳	**Toxicity**	No reported toxicity
✳	**Also known as**	California sunlight, cup of gold, golden poppy

How to spot • You'll find California poppies thriving in full sunshine and poor soil. The foliage is blueish-green in colour and has a feathery appearance. It is branching and highly divided. The flowers are small and upright, measuring a maximum of 5cm in diameter. The most striking feature of this plant is the flower colour – a glowing, bright orange, though new varieties are now available in lemon yellow, pink and red.

Perks • As with most self-seeders, if you like the flowers, why wouldn't you want more of them? Leaving them be is a low-maintenance way to fill an outdoor space with your preferred flowers, perfect for busy gardeners. And if you've inherited a patch of poor-quality soil, Californian poppies will spread quickly and fill your plot with vivid colour. The seedlings are easy to remove by hand if desired.

Pitfalls • On the whole, these carefree plants have few downsides although, as noted, they will take over in bare soil. Aphids can be a problem, and – thanks to their Californian roots – the plants don't like soggy or rich soils.

Did you know? • This poppy has been California's official state flower since 1903.

Campanula (*Campanula portenschlagiana* and *Campanula poscharskyana*)

Greenery Nursery

✳	**Flowers**	May to November
✳	**Foliage**	Evergreen
✳	**Height**	50cm
✳	**Spread**	50cm
✳	**Preferred conditions**	Sun, dappled shade
✳	**Origin**	Europe
✳	**Toxicity**	No reported toxicity
✳	**Also known as**	Creeping bellflower, climbing bellflower, Dalmatian bellflower, trailing bellflower, Serbian bellflower, wall bellflower

Tim Green

How to spot • Look for campanula growing in the narrow crevices of brick walls and pavements or spilling over rockeries or low walls. These trailing plants form generous mats of foliage and flowers, with the crinkled, evergreen leaves persisting throughout the winter. The flowers are petite and purple, in the shape of a five-pointed star, and bloom en masse.

Perks • Campanulas are easy to grow and care for, as long as they get some sun, and flower from late spring right through to autumn. In mild winters, they can even flower well into December. Bonus points for the fact that the evergreen foliage provides a welcome pop of green all year round.

Pitfalls • Without any cutting back, the foliage can fall on the straggly side, which more meticulous gardeners might find unsightly. And this is a plant best left to run free, allowing it to spread merrily over walls and rockeries – so not the best choice for anyone wedded to a strict planting scheme.

Did you know? • The trailing or creeping bellflower (*Campanula poscharskyana*) is very similar in appearance to the wall bellflower, although with slightly paler flowers, and is an equally lovely addition to walls and raised beds.

Canterbury bells (*Campanula medium*)

Author

Tanaka Juuyoh

✳	**Flowers**	May to July
✳	**Foliage**	Deciduous
✳	**Height**	1m
✳	**Spread**	50cm
✳	**Preferred conditions**	Sun, light shade
✳	**Origin**	Europe
✳	**Toxicity**	No reported toxicity
✳	**Also known as**	Coventry bells, cup and saucer, fair-in-sight, gingerbread bells, lady's nightcap, Mercury's violets, St Thomas's bell

How to spot • Canterbury bells are a biennial plant, which means they grow foliage in the first year before blooming in their second. However, their tendency to seed themselves about means you'll often have flowers from one or another plant every year. In the first year, you'll notice a low-growing rosette of green leaves with serrated edges. In the second, the plant sends up flower spikes of up to a metre adorned with bell-shaped purple, pink or white flowers.

Perks • Bees love the flowers, as they do almost all bell-shaped blooms. The flowers of Canterbury bells are also long-lasting, both on the plant and in a vase.

Pitfalls • This plant's self-seeding nature can create extra work if you're not keen on a thicket of Canterbury bells. Nonetheless, it's easy to weed out any unwanted seedlings by hand.

Did you know? • It's unclear how Canterbury bells acquired their name, but a connection to the Kentish locale is assumed: one theory suggests pilgrims picked the flowers on their way to the city's cathedral.

Comfrey (*Symphytum officinale*)

Bryony Bowie

✳	**Flowers**	May to July
✳	**Foliage**	Deciduous
✳	**Height**	1.5m
✳	**Spread**	1.5m
✳	**Preferred conditions**	Sun, partial shade
✳	**Origin**	Europe, Asia
✳	**Toxicity**	No reported toxicity
✳	**Also known as**	Boneset, knitbone, Quaker's comfrey

How to spot • You'll find comfrey growing on allotments, waste ground and in damp places. It has long, hairy, bristled leaves – a little like foxglove foliage (p. 74) – and grows in large clumps. Between May and July, clusters of small, bell-shaped flowers – white with a tinge of mauve – appear, visited often by bees and other pollinators.

Perks • A patch of comfrey is a stroke of luck for organic gardeners: the plant's leaves can be brewed into a nutrient-rich fertiliser or added to compost to speed up the decomposition process.

Pitfalls • In gardens, it can be a bit of a nuisance as it spreads by seed quickly and can regrow from tiny sections of root – but it's difficult to remove fully, so is perhaps best appreciated and utilised for its abundance of nutrients.

Did you know? • Some of the plant's other names – boneset, and knitbone – hint at its healing powers. Comfrey has a long folk history of being used to treat injured or broken bones and modern research has backed up this tradition. While it won't fix a mangled limb on its own, the plant does contain allantoin – a substance that aids the growth of new cells – and anti-inflammatories.

Cornflower (*Centaurea cyanus*)

Author

* **Flowers**	June to August
* **Foliage**	Deciduous
* **Height**	1m
* **Spread**	50cm
* **Preferred conditions**	Sun
* **Origin**	Europe
* **Toxicity**	No reported toxicity
* **Also known as**	Bachelor's buttons, barbecue, beaver, blawort, bluebottle, bluets, blue blaw, blue bonnets, blue bow, blue poppy, blue sailors, blue tops, break-your-spectacles, brushes, bunk, cornbottle, French pink, happy skies, haw dods, hurtsickle, ragged robin, ragged sailor, witches bells

How to spot • Cornflowers are an indigenous UK plant, once a common sight in farmers' cornfields, but the widespread use of herbicides means they are now rare in the wild. These days you're more likely to spot them in gardens and parks, as they are often included in packets of mixed wildflower seed. The stems are long, thin, and spindly, and the leaves nothing to write home about, but once the flowering season arrives, you'll notice domed, black-veined buds turning to intensely blue flowers that measure 2.5–5cm in diameter.

Perks • Cornflowers have been designated a 'Priority Species' in the UK since 2010 as their numbers have declined dramatically over past decades, so if you're fortunate enough to spot them growing of their own accord on your plot, count yourself (and the bees) lucky. They're also simple to grow from seed.

Pitfalls • There's little bad to say about cornflowers – perhaps the only pitfall, if you can call it such, is that they're so rarely spotted in the wild. Modern cultivars with large, ruffled blooms may also struggle to hold their own weight, resulting in droopy stems (though on the plus side, that means more to bring inside!).

Did you know? • Cornflowers, like many native plants, have a sprawling history of herbal use in the UK. One of the plant's colloquial titles – the peculiarly charming 'break-your-spectacles' – holds clues to its use for treating visual problems. Homeopaths of the past thought it could be used to heal poor eyesight, presumably leading the cured patient to smash up their spectacles in surprise or delight.

Cyclamen (*Cyclamen* spp.)

✳	**Flowers**	October to December
✳	**Foliage**	Deciduous
✳	**Height**	50cm
✳	**Spread**	50cm
✳	**Preferred conditions**	Dappled shade, partial shade, shade
✳	**Origin**	Europe, the Middle East
✳	**Toxicity**	Toxic to humans, cats, dogs and horses
✳	**Also known as**	Persian violet, sow bread

Zane Priedite

How to spot • You may know cyclamen as a houseplant – tender varieties are often sold in florists, supermarkets and garden centres for indoor enjoyment in the depths of winter. But hardier varieties also exist, with ivy-leaved *Cyclamen hederifolium* naturalised in Britain. This plant, like other types of cyclamen, has silvery-green, rounded foliage with snakeskin-like mottling on the upper sides of the leaves. The flowers of common ivy-leaved cyclamen are a bright medium pink, but cultivated varieties are available with white, red and purple flowers.

Perks • Gem-like flowers with an interesting shape – as though the flowers are facing backwards – and eye-catching leaf patterns make cyclamen a welcome sight in late autumn and winter. They are particularly radiant in the snow, with their polished leaves and luminous flowers beaming among the white.

Pitfalls • Mice and squirrels love the tubers almost as much as they do crocuses (p. 52), so you may sometimes find your cyclamen have been dug up. Unfortunately, pollinators don't share their enthusiasm. Cyclamen's wildlife benefits are lacking. Plants in sunny, dry areas may also suffer in hot summers.

Did you know? • Cyclamen has been grown in the UK for hundreds of years – it is listed in the first ever Oxford Botanic Gardens catalogue, published in 1648.

  WHAT IS THAT PLANT?

Elephant's ears *(Bergenia* spp.)

Author

Sebastian Rittau

✳ Flowers	February to April
✳ Foliage	Evergreen
✳ Height	60cm
✳ Spread	1.5m
✳ Preferred conditions	Sun, partial shade, shade
✳ Origin	Europe, Asia
✳ Toxicity	Toxic to dogs
✳ Also known as	Bergenia, pigsqueak

How to spot • The clue is in the name – the shiny, glossy green leaves of this common garden plant are shaped like elephant's ears. The foliage is evergreen, so leaves can be spotted all year round. In late winter and early spring, straight stalks of pink, white or purple flowers rise from the foliage.

Perks • Elephant's ears are hardy little plants, having evolved in areas of Russia, China and Mongolia where extremes of temperature are a given. This means the plants are pretty unfussy, adapting to shade, sun, drought or downpours. They also grow well in most soil types and need little aftercare once planted, or inherited, making them a good bet for beginners.

Pitfalls • If your elephant's ears have been planted in a spot where they receive harsh sun in the afternoon, you may notice their leaves are scalded by the sunlight. Otherwise, common complaints are that the leaves look untidy for much of the year and they flower for only a short period – which some consider a poor payoff given that the evergreen leaves must be looked at all year.

Did you know? • At the famous Gravel Garden planted by the late, great plantswoman Beth Chatto in Essex, bergenias are a key anchor of the drought-resistant planting scheme.

Feverfew (*Tanacetum parthenium*)

✳ Flowers	July to October
✳ Foliage	Deciduous
✳ Height	50cm
✳ Spread	50cm
✳ Preferred conditions	Sun, dappled shade
✳ Origin	Europe, Asia
✳ Toxicity	No reported toxicity
✳ Also known as	Bachelor's buttons, featherfew, featherfoil, maids, pale maids, tansy

How to spot • This perennial plant returns year after year, sprinkling its offspring merrily through borders and beds. It has a mildly fragrant scent and feathery foliage with scalloped borders, like the edges of a shell or a vintage tablecloth. The leaves are green with a slightly yellow tinge. Feverfew flowers are similar in colour and shape to other daisies (p. 190) and chrysanthemums (p. 22), with yellow centres and white petals. Nowadays many double varieties with subtler colouring are also available.

Perks • Masses of sunny flower heads, visually interesting foliage, loved by hoverflies, self-seeding without you having to lift a finger – feverfew has much to recommend it. It's often found in herb gardens for its alleged ability to ease migraines.

Andrey Zharkikh

Pitfalls • Perhaps its tendency to self-seed widely, but it's easily pulled up or rehomed if it spreads where you don't want it. And besides its biggest fan, the hoverfly, it sadly has little value to UK wildlife.

Did you know? • Feverfew's name hints at its history: in the era before modern medicine, it was used to alleviate high temperatures.

Forget-me-not (*Myosotis* spp.)

✳	Flowers	April to June
✳	Foliage	Semi-evergreen
✳	Height	50cm
✳	Spread	50cm
✳	Preferred conditions	Dappled shade, partial shade
✳	Origin	Europe, Asia, North America, mountains of the tropics
✳	Toxicity	No reported toxicity
✳	Also known as	Love-me, mouse ear

How to spot • The forget-me-not throws up delicate blue flowers with a yellow centre, emerging from pinkish-purple buds into clouds of periwinkle-coloured blooms from April until mid-summer. Look for light grey–green leaves with an oval shape and a velvety texture.

Perks • Forget-me-nots are worth keeping around for their ability to fill awkward gaps in borders in the springtime and are popular as edging for borders and paths. Their clouds of baby blue blooms lend a relaxed feel to an outdoor space. And if you change your mind later, they're easy to pull up by hand.

Katrin Hauf

Pitfalls • As the name indicates, you won't forget about forget-me-nots – not least because while you might start out with a handful of plants, the next year you'll have gained many more. They will fail to thrive in dry conditions, and can be prone to unsightly fungal diseases that leave patches on the foliage.

Did you know? • There are many different varieties of forget-me-nots, including the water forget-me-not (*Myosotis scorpioides*), which thrives in ponds and around the edges of shallow water.

Foxglove (*Digitalis* spp.)

Author

✳ **Flowers**	June to September
✳ **Foliage**	Deciduous
✳ **Height**	2m
✳ **Spread**	50cm
✳ **Preferred conditions**	Sun, partial shade, full shade
✳ **Origin**	Europe, Asia, Africa
✳ **Toxicity**	Toxic to humans, cats, dogs and horses
✳ **Also known as**	Bloody bells, bloody finger, cow flop, dead man's bells, dog's lugs, dragon's mouth, fairy bells, fairy fingers, fairy gloves, fairy thimbles, fairy's cap, fairy's petticoat, fairy's thimble, finger flower, flap dock, folk's gloves, fox finger, gloves of Mary, lady's fingers, lady's gloves, lady's thimble, lion's mouth, lusmore, lustmore, pop dock, thimble finger, thimble flower, throat root, witches' bells, witches' fingers, witches' gloves, witches' thimbles

How to spot • Foxglove flowers come in a variety of purple, pink, red, cream and white shades, but all varieties share bell-shaped flowers with delicately spotted throats. Furry leaves sit in a rose-like clump at the base of the plant with floral spires towering above. Foxgloves are most likely to be found in dappled shade – recreating the forest conditions they evolved with.

Perks • The foxglove's early summer flowers will brighten up the garden in late May and June once the spring bulbs are dying back but late summer perennials are yet to reach their peak bloom. The striking spikes of flowers are particularly useful for adding visual interest and light to the back of a border, with some varieties reaching up to 2m in height.

Author

Pitfalls • Just one plant can produce more than a million seeds, so – like most of the plants in this chapter – foxgloves will spread quickly in the right conditions. If you share your outdoor space with particularly inquisitive children or pets, remember that all parts of the foxglove plant are highly toxic to humans, cats and dogs if ingested.

Did you know? • Foxgloves are extremely poisonous to humans, yet the drug digitalis contained in the plant – the same chemical that can prove fatal – is used in heart medicines. At too high a dose, this substance can cause the heart to stop beating, but at lower levels, it can stabilise heart rate and circulation.

Grape hyacinth (*Muscari* spp.)

✶	**Flowers**	April to May
✶	**Foliage**	Deciduous
✶	**Height**	50cm
✶	**Spread**	10cm
✶	**Preferred conditions**	Sun, dappled shade, partial shade
✶	**Origin**	the Mediterranean
✶	**Toxicity**	No reported toxicity
✶	**Also known as**	Grape flower, muscari, starch hyacinth

Author

How to spot • This pint-sized plant pops up all over the place in gardens, churchyards, and public parks, so you may well find it on your patch of land or out and about. These bulbs are dormant for much of the year, but in autumn, their thin, green leaves appear above ground – a little like upright shoelaces. You'll have to wait until April and May for the flowers, which arrive in a profusion of tiny, rounded clusters. The dainty blooms, traditionally lapis blue but also sometimes white, lilac or pink, are shaped like an upright thimble and each minuscule petal is spherical like a grape.

Perks • Grape hyacinths need little care and brighten up gardens in April and May. They are not vulnerable to pests or diseases, and make excellent ground cover to suppress weeds under trees. If they spread more widely than preferred, they can easily be dug up and contained in a pot to stem their onward march. The flowers offer an early spring supply of nectar to hungry pollinators.

Pitfalls • In very rich soil, grape hyacinths tend to put out more leaf than flower. If you find that's the case on your plot, consider moving them to somewhere with stony soil, a gravelled area or container.

Did you know? • The botanical epithet *Muscari* is related to the Greek word for musk, referring to the flower's subtle scent.

Hollyhock (*Alcea rosea*)

✳	Flowers	July to September
✳	Foliage	Deciduous
✳	Height	2.5m
✳	Spread	1.2m
✳	Preferred conditions	Sun
✳	Origin	China
✳	Toxicity	No reported toxicity

How to spot • A common sight in seaside gardens, hollyhocks flower on tall spires and have saucer-shaped blooms that come in a wealth of colours ranging from marshmallow pink to deepest red as well as shades of purple, yellow and cream. They grow to at least a metre in height but are often far taller. The spade-shaped leaves are rough to the touch and often sport reddish-brown blotches. You will likely notice the resemblance to mallow (p. 189) flowers, which belong to the same plant family.

Perks • There's little reason not to enjoy these striking flowers unless they're shading out lower plants, given that they can grow to over two metres tall. They are quintessential cottage garden plants, their towering silhouettes offering colour, height and radiance.

Author

Pitfalls • Hollyhocks are prone to rust, a fungal disease that leaves those unsightly bronzed spots on the foliage. This can be treated in the early stages by removing and destroying the affected leaves. The foliage can also grow to over a metre wide, so providing ample space is vital.

Did you know? • When hollyhock rust first spread from South America to Europe, hollyhocks vanished almost into oblivion in Britain for about three decades before coming back into fashion in the 1930s.

Lady's mantle (*Alchemilla mollis*)

Author

✱	**Flowers**	May to August
✱	**Foliage**	Deciduous
✱	**Height**	50cm
✱	**Spread**	50cm
✱	**Preferred conditions**	Sun, dappled shade, partial shade
✱	**Origin**	Europe, Asia
✱	**Toxicity**	No reported toxicity
✱	**Also known as**	Garden lady's mantle, woman's best friend

How to spot • Look for bright green leaves with crinkly edges that are particularly distinctive in the rain, when they catch and hold raindrops like upturned umbrellas. They are said to look like a woman's cloak clutched around the shoulders – hence the common name. The lime green flowers are small, but vivid in colour and frothingly generous. They turn to brown seed heads by August.

Perks • Green flowers, especially of this zesty, energising shade, are few and far between, making lady's mantle something of a collector's item. It also provides welcome sustenance for the red carpet moth caterpillar, while parched butterflies and insects can drink rain water from its saucer-like foliage.

Pitfalls • The drawback to growing *Alchemilla mollis* is how widely and freely it self-seeds and spreads. Once it's established on a patch, weary gardeners may find themselves digging up seedling after seedling where they are not wanted. However, that does mean once you have one plant, you'll never need to plant or buy another!

Did you know? • Perhaps because of its name, the plant has long had feminine connotations. In the past it was given to expectant mothers to prevent miscarriage.

Lemon balm (*Melissa officinalis*)

✳ **Flowers**	June to September
✳ **Foliage**	Deciduous
✳ **Height**	1m
✳ **Spread**	50cm
✳ **Preferred conditions**	Sun, dappled shade, partial shade
✳ **Origin**	the Mediterranean, Asia
✳ **Toxicity**	No reported toxicity
✳ **Also known as**	Balm, balm leaf, balm oil plant, bee balm. cure-all, dropsywort, honey plant, lemon mint, melissa, pimentary, sweet balm, sweet Mary, tea balm

How to spot • Pick a leaf and rub it between your fingers – lemon balm gives off a strong citrusy aroma. The oval leaves are softly furred and gently scalloped around the edges. Small white or purple flowers appear on leafy spikes in the summer.

Perks • A patch of lemon balm outside the back door or perched in a window box provides a heady thrill, so long as you like the smell. Pollinators will also pay many a visit to its scented blooms. Leaves can be picked and soaked in boiling water for a homemade herbal tea. In fact, its culinary uses are almost endless, whether to flavour icing or roasted meats.

Bryony Bowie

Pitfalls • Like mint, lemon balm can get out of hand in open soil and is best contained in a pot, where you can still enjoy its fragrance without the fear it will take over. And some find the smell off-putting – but you'll have to take a good sniff to find out!

Did you know? • The plant's genus name *Melissa* derives from a form of the Greek word for 'honey bee' or 'bee leaf'. The pollinators seem to agree!

Love-in-a-mist (*Nigella damascena*)

✳	**Flowers**	June to August
✳	**Foliage**	Deciduous
✳	**Height**	50cm
✳	**Spread**	50cm
✳	**Preferred conditions**	Sun, dappled shade
✳	**Origin**	Europe, North Africa, Asia
✳	**Toxicity**	No reported toxicity
✳	**Also known as**	Bird's nest, blue spiderflower, chase-the-devil, devil in the bush, garden fennel, Jack in prison, Jack in the green, Katherine's flower, kiss-me-twice-before-I-rise, lady in the bower, love-in-a-puzzle, love-in-a-tangle, nigella, St Catherine's flower

  WHAT IS THAT PLANT?

Author

How to spot • The green foliage of love-in-a-mist is frond-like and frothy, creating a bushy overall appearance. The single flowers appear at the top of long, thin stalks. Blooms are generally blue but can also be white, pink, purple or a mixture of these shades. Each flower measures about four centimetres in diameter and can be single or double-layered. As the flower goes to seed, unusual seed heads form that look like small, inflated balloons.

Perks • There are few flowers quite like these, with their delicate bracts and ethereal appearance. They make pretty cut flowers, while the nectar-rich blooms attract bees and other pollinators. The plant will spread thickly close to where the previous flowers set seed, which is great for low-effort gardening.

Pitfalls • If you'd rather it didn't spread, remove the seed heads or deadhead flowers before the plant has a chance to set seed.

Did you know? • Although nigella flowers are edible, the related plant *Nigella sativa* is the source of the nigella seeds used in Indian cuisine.

Lungwort (*Pulmonaria officinalis*)

Karen Hine

✱	**Flowers**	April to June
✱	**Foliage**	Deciduous
✱	**Height**	50cm
✱	**Spread**	50cm
✱	**Preferred conditions**	Partial shade, full shade
✱	**Origin**	Europe, Asia
✱	**Toxicity**	No reported toxicity
✱	**Also known as**	Bedlam cowslip, beggar's basket, bugloss cowslip, Jerusalem cowslip, lady's cowslip, Mary's honeysuckle, soldiers and sailors, spotted dog

How to spot • You'll usually find this plant thriving in the shade, where it can provide ground cover, although established plants may also be found in the sun. Lungwort's oval leaves are speckled with silver markings and have a furry texture. In spring, petite tubular flowers emerge – in pink, white, or blue. These change colour after pollination, and it is common to see more than one flower colour on the same plant.

Perks • Although lungwort self-seeds, it does so gently, with a conscientious courtesy that means it rarely gets out of hand. I find it a charming little plant, with its changing flower colours and attractive speckled leaves that persist throughout the summer.

Pitfalls • If you're planning a garden with a rigid colour scheme, its chameleon flowers may throw up issues. The leaves are also susceptible to powdery mildew.

Did you know? • Both the Latin name *Pulmonaria* and the common term lungwort refers to the way the plant's leaves and tubular flowers resemble human lungs.

Mexican fleabane (*Erigeron karvinskianus*)

Author

✳	**Flowers**	May to October
✳	**Foliage**	Deciduous
✳	**Height**	50cm
✳	**Spread**	1m
✳	**Preferred conditions**	Sun
✳	**Origin**	Mexico, Central America, South America
✳	**Toxicity**	No reported toxicity
✳	**Also known as**	Latin American fleabane, little buttons, Mexican daisy

How to spot • This relative of the common daisy is distinguished by the pink-edged petals of its dainty white flowers. It forms low-growing mats of green foliage and flowers, and often pops up in patio cracks, low walls and rockeries. It likes well-drained soil, which is why it gravitates towards gravel, pavement and gaps in dry stone walls. You'll find it thriving in full sunshine and struggling elsewhere.

Perks • Cheery flowers between May and October that tumble over walls and rockeries, tuck themselves into the tiniest crevices, and bestow a joyful, carefree feel to any garden. One gardener's weed is another's worship – it's now widely sold in garden centres and included in designer planting schemes.

Pitfalls • Fleabane is a polarising plant among gardeners – loved by some, loathed by others. For those in the latter camp, its squatter-like tendencies make it a nuisance in more formal planting schemes.

Did you know? • Although its benefits in this regard have never been conclusively proven, fleabane was thought to repel fleas and bed bugs – although it shouldn't be relied upon!

Mint (*Mentha* spp.)

✳	**Flowers**	June to September
✳	**Foliage**	Deciduous
✳	**Height**	1m
✳	**Spread**	1.5m
✳	**Preferred conditions**	Sun, partial shade
✳	**Origin**	Europe, Asia, Africa
✳	**Toxicity**	Toxic to cats, dogs and horses
✳	**Also known as**	Common mint, garden mint

How to spot • You'll probably smell mint before you see it: the familiar menthol-scented leaves of this culinary herb will be familiar to most. There are many varieties of mint, but the majority have soft green foliage, oval leaves and small white or purple flowers from midsummer. Some have variegated leaves. Due to its sly spreading skills, you might find it popping up in places you don't expect it, but it grows at its wily best in loose soil where it can spread out its roots.

Perks • That classic peppy aroma, a supply of fresh mint tea, and myriad other culinary applications – mint has a lot going for it. Bees and other pollinators are fanatical about the flowers, too. And nowadays there are many intriguing varieties, from chocolate-scented to pineapple mint.

Pitfalls • There's a reason why gardeners are advised to grow mint in a pot – this dogged herb spreads quickly via its spreading roots. Once you've got mint in open soil, you'll likely find it popping up there for eternity. If you're still keen on planting mint in the ground, bury your plant in a container to restrict the spread of its roots.

Did you know? • Imagine mint and you'll probably think of toothpaste, yet it's only been the conventional flavouring for our oral ablutions since the 1800s, when manufacturers started using it to mask the taste of the other ingredients.

Thiago Falcão

Nasturtium (*Tropaeolum majus*)

✳	**Flowers**	June to September
✳	**Foliage**	Deciduous
✳	**Height**	2.5m
✳	**Spread**	2.5m
✳	**Preferred conditions**	Sun
✳	**Origin**	Mexico, Central America, South America
✳	**Toxicity**	No reported toxicity
✳	**Also known as**	Capuchin cress, Indian cress

How to spot • This scrambling plant, which trails across the ground if unsupported, has large leaves balanced on skinny stems like swaying green parasols, marked by white veins that extend from a central point. Turn over a leaf from midsummer onwards and you're likely to find an abundance of aphids, which are especially fond of feeding on the sap. Some varieties have variegated leaves. Funnel-shaped flowers are typically orange or yellow, with five petals, although pink, red and white varieties have also been developed.

Author

Perks • Nasturtium can be a useful plant in the garden or vegetable patch, its peppery leaves a midsummer alternative to rocket, which tends to go to seed in the June heat. The flowers are also edible, and the seed pods can be pickled like capers. You can also use it as a companion plant to lure aphids away from your prized vegetables.

Pitfalls • The siren call of nasturtiums to aphids and caterpillars does have a downside – particularly severely affected plants can begin to falter under their attack, turning yellow and limp, or dying back entirely. Caterpillar-induced holes in the leaves also make the plant look a bit of a mess in a border. And with a potential height and spread of 2.5m, choose your location wisely.

Did you know? • Nasturtium derives from the Latin words for 'nose' and 'twist' – smell the peppery, spiced leaves and you'll swiftly understand why.

Periwinkle (*Vinca* spp.)

Eleanor Burfitt

✶	**Flowers**	March to October
✶	**Foliage**	Evergreen
✶	**Height**	50cm
✶	**Spread**	2m
✶	**Preferred conditions**	Sun, partial shade, full shade
✶	**Origin**	Europe, Africa, Asia
✶	**Toxicity**	Toxic to humans, cats, dogs and horses
✶	**Also known as**	Band plant, creeping myrtle, cut-finger, flower of death, grave myrtle, ground myrtle, large periwinkle, sorcerer's violet

How to spot • Periwinkles are low-growing, evergreen plants that sprawl across the ground in shady areas. The glossy, dark green or variegated leaves are oval-shaped and grow on long, creeping stems. Distinguish via the flowers, which have a distinctive, five-petalled shape and a white centre. Traditionally an arresting shade of glowing lilac, white cultivars have also been developed. *Vinca minor* and *Vinca major* (the lesser and greater periwinkles, respectively) are the most common types in British gardens.

Perks • Periwinkles can be quite useful garden plants for tricky shady spots you're not quite sure what to do with. Its purple flowers twinkle in areas lacking light and under trees, it makes a superb ground cover plant to suppress the growth of other weeds.

Pitfalls • The greater periwinkle (*Vinca major*) can metastasize quickly when it finds the right conditions, so treat it with caution. A spread of two metres is not to be sniffed at and its foliage will send down roots wherever and whenever it comes into contact with the soil. It's also highly poisonous to both humans and many common pets.

Did you know? • In the Middle Ages, condemned prisoners were sent to the gallows with wreaths of periwinkle around their necks due to the plant's enduring association with death (not least thanks to its lethal qualities).

Pot marigold (*Calendula officinalis*)

✳	**Flowers**	June to November
✳	**Foliage**	Deciduous
✳	**Height**	50cm
✳	**Spread**	50cm
✳	**Preferred conditions**	Sun
✳	**Origin**	Europe, Asia
✳	**Toxicity**	No reported toxicity
✳	**Also known as**	Calendula, common marigold, English marigold, golds, goldins, Jack-on-horseback, marybuds, Mary's gold, Scotch marigold

Author

How to spot • The soft, slightly furred leaves are simple, elongated ovals and free from markings or much visual interest. Marigold flowers are usually a bright orange or yellow – although more muted shades have also been bred – and measure between 5-7cm in diameter. Like other self-seeders, calendula may be found growing in pavement cracks or between patio pavers.

Perks • Marigolds have an incredibly long-flowering period, sometimes blooming well into the British winter – a welcome burst of colour when the landscape is brown and grey. They're also a useful companion plant, often planted between tomatoes and beans to repel pests, which tend to be drawn to marigolds instead of your prized fruit and vegetables.

Pitfalls • That nimble knack for attracting pests? Sometimes pot marigolds do too good a job, and you will find your plants covered in aphids – not the prettiest sight. The leaves are also prone to powdery mildew.

Did you know? • The deep hue of calendula was used as an edible dye in centuries past, often to colour butter and rice.

Sea holly (*Eryngium* spp.)

Gareth Williams

✱	**Flowers**	July to September
✱	**Foliage**	Deciduous
✱	**Height**	1m
✱	**Spread**	50cm
✱	**Preferred conditions**	Sun
✱	**Origin**	Europe
✱	**Toxicity**	No reported toxicity
✱	**Also known as**	Blue thistle, seaside thistle

How to spot • The most common varieties in gardens are united by their blueish-purple, metallic foliage and statement-making, thistle-like flowers. The flower's central petals are encircled by a distinctive collar of angular foliage, a bit like a Tudor-style ruff. Sea holly can resemble the globe thistle (*Echinops* spp., p. 28), but the latter has much rounder flowers without the ruff of foliage, and green leaves.

Perks • Sea holly in a garden makes a striking spectacle and will flourish on bright, sunny, south-facing plots. The purple foliage is certainly eye-catching – and not just to humans. Bees and butterflies are big fans, too.

Pitfalls • These plants are quite picky – they won't thrive in shady areas or in heavy, rich soils like clay. They're also prickly to the touch, like the more common ordinary holly, so keep away from roving young hands.

Did you know? • The wild form of sea holly (*Eryngium maritimum*), which grows on the coast and has dusky green foliage, is edible – its roots were dug up, coated in sugar and sold as candied treats in times past.

Snapdragon (*Antirrhinum majus*)

S. Tsuchiya

✳ **Flowers**	June to October
✳ **Foliage**	Deciduous
✳ **Height**	90cm
✳ **Spread**	50cm
✳ **Preferred conditions**	Sun, dappled shade
✳ **Origin**	north America, the Mediterranean
✳ **Toxicity**	No reported toxicity
✳ **Also known as**	Calf's mouth, calf-snout, dog's mouth, dragon's mouth, lion's mouth, lion's snap, tiger's mouth, toad's mouth

How to spot • This plant's dark green leaves are simple and inconspicuous – the flowers are what really catches the eye. Each individual flower is lipped, providing a landing surface for hungry bees to rest on. Flowers are generally pink, red, white, yellow, purple, or orange. To identify, press the top and bottom lip of the flower together, then release – the petals will snap open like a dragon's mouth. Their prolific self-seeding habits means you'll often find them in unexpected places, such as patio and pavement cracks, kerbs, and gutters.

Perks • The frilly florets are a favourite of florists, with the blooms lasting about a week in a vase. If my sister and I were anything to go by, children will love playing with the dragon-like flowers.

Matthew Bellmare

They're also attractive to bees and can provide nectar – as well as a visual feast for the humans frequenting your plot – for several months.

Pitfalls • My green-thumbed grandfather has a saying: 'Plant one and you'll always have snapdragons.' Personally, I wouldn't mind having snapdragons popping up all over for ever and a day, but that's a matter of taste. Small volunteer seedlings are quite easy to pull up if you don't fancy them. Like hollyhocks (*Alcea rosea*, p. 77) snapdragons are prone to rust, which results in reddish-brown splotches on the leaves.

Did you know? • The Latin name *Antirrhinum* translates as 'like a snout', referencing the nose-shaped flowers.

Sweet rocket (*Hesperis matronalis*)

Author

✳	**Flowers**	May to June
✳	**Foliage**	Deciduous
✳	**Height**	1m
✳	**Spread**	50cm
✳	**Preferred conditions**	Sun, dappled shade, partial shade
✳	**Origin**	Europe
✳	**Toxicity**	No reported toxicity
✳	**Also known as**	Dame's violet, damask violet, dame's wort, dame's rocket, night rocket, night violet, night-scented violet, summer lilac

How to spot • When in flower, lean in and check the scent: sweet rocket is one of the headiest floral fragrances out there. The foliage is green and slightly furry, with oval-shaped leaves. The aromatic flowers come in varying shades of purple, from dark aubergine to lilac, and nowadays also white. They are held in rounded clusters at the top of long stems – think of the silhouette of a feather duster (but with a far nicer smell!). This plant is technically a biennial – growing foliage in one season, flowering the next – but can sometimes last for several years and seeds about everywhere except in very dry conditions, so you may notice it popping up even if you didn't plant it recently.

Perks • Soak in its scent, at its peak in the evening, and those vividly coloured flowers. It plays host to the caterpillars of several butterfly species and is appreciated by bees, moths and butterflies. The plant has a relaxed appearance so looks most at home on wilder patches, allotments and in informal borders.

Pitfalls • Flowering briefly in May and June (though with such abundance!), sweet rocket's blooming season isn't the longest – although to my mind, it more than makes up for that with its other virtues.

Did you know? • Sweet rocket is a member of the *Brassicaceae* family – the same group that includes cabbages and broccoli.

Verbena (*Verbena bonariensis*)

✳ Flowers	Mid to late summer
✳ Foliage	Deciduous
✳ Height	1.8m
✳ Spread	90cm
✳ Preferred conditions	Sun
✳ Origin	South America
✳ Toxicity	No reported toxicity
✳ Also known as	Argentinian vervain, purple top, purpletop vervain, tall verbena, vervain

How to spot • This on-trend plant has enjoyed the spotlight in recent years, so you may have spotted it in municipal plantings or in other people's gardens. The branching stems are inconspicuous – slender and dark forest green – and the compact but ruffly flowers that sit atop them are a vivid purple shade, similar to lavender.

Author

Perks • Verbena is loved by bees and butterflies and provides glowing colour right up until the first frosts. Thanks to its spreading tendency, huge drifts can form – and it's en masse that this delicate plant really shines. It is best to leave the stems and flower heads over winter too, to protect the plant from cold weather, which means it provides structural winter interest in the garden. It is frost-hardy to -10°C only for short periods, but self-seeded offspring mean you don't need to worry too much about losing the parent plants to the chill.

Pitfalls • It self-seeds readily in the right conditions, so you may want to thin the plants it so readily produces or choose its position wisely. Its stiff stems are rather bristly – something I've learned the hard way cutting back plants with bare forearms on my allotment – so long sleeves when handling at close range are recommended.

Did you know? • In America the plant's common name is purpletop vervain or tall verbena. Despite its lavish and sudden popularity on this side of the pond in the last decade, the cultivar is yet to be given a common title in the UK.

Wallflower (*Erysimum* spp.)

Author

Perennial (everlasting) wallflower. Judy Dean

✳	**Flowers**	March to April
✳	**Foliage**	Semi-evergreen
✳	**Height**	1m
✳	**Spread**	1m
✳	**Preferred conditions**	Sun, dappled shade, partial shade
✳	**Origin**	the Mediterranean
✳	**Toxicity**	No reported toxicity
✳	**Also known as**	Blister cress, cheiranthus

How to spot • Wallflowers are short-lived perennials that are usually treated as biennials in the UK, so you'll see foliage one year and flowers the next. Leaves are grey–green, long, thin tapered to a point at the outer edge. The flowers, which appear in early spring, are scented and produced in abundance in bouquet-like clusters above the leaves. They come in a wide variety of colours, from dark mauve to fiery orange. As self-seeders you'll find wallflowers happily thriving in the unlikeliest of places, like cracks between pavers and kerb edges.

Perks • While they may be found growing in hard-to-reach places, wallflowers are prized for their early spring colour in a vivid array of shades. Breeders have now created varieties that last for more than a year or two, so it is worth seeking these out for a lower-maintenance option. Popular with pollinators, they don't mind the type of soil they grow in and have a lovely perfume.

Pitfalls • As many wallflowers are not known for their longevity, the flowers are unlikely to last for more than a year or two. That means you'll have to keep resowing or planting. Thankfully, the self-seeding habits of most wallflowers mean that the plants will often do that job for you!

Did you know? • The term 'wallflower', used to describe an introverted person who prefers to stand off to the side, is inspired by the plant, which is often seen growing alongside or in walls, almost out of sight.

Shrubs, grasses, trees & climbers

S hrubs often form the backbone of a garden or cultivated outdoor space, providing structure or screening. Some cover the ground; others grow up walls or alongside fences. Most shrubs and climbers are multi-stemmed and live for at least three years. Trees found in gardens can be small or large, with a single trunk and a canopy of branches at the crown. Trees are longer-lived than shrubs, with most surviving a quarter of a century as a minimum. And, of course, shrubs, climbers and trees are everywhere, not just in our gardens, but also on the streets we walk, alongside railways, in public parks and hedgerows.

Shrubs and trees, like self-seeders, can be a blessing for novice or time-pressed gardeners. As well as providing colour and delicious fragrance during multiple seasons, the woody stems and shape ensure winter structure and something to look at when most perennial plants have died back for the year. Aside from pruning and perhaps a feed once or twice a year, most shrubs are low-maintenance plants that don't need much special care to thrive. That makes them especially useful to busy gardeners, not to mention local councils!

Identifying shrubs, climbing shrubs and trees can be tricky, given the sheer variety available. I certainly find recognising shrubby specimens a little more difficult than common perennials and wildflowers, which often have more distinctive flowers. Paying attention to the blossoms, leaf shape, colour and texture, the bark, and the way that the woody stems grow are all good starting points when looking to identify shrubs, climbers and trees. The following chapter lists some of the most popular and widely available shrubs, trees and climbers in Britain alongside, again, some of my personal favourites.

Bamboo (Various)

Author

✱	**Foliage**	Evergreen
✱	**Height**	20m
✱	**Spread**	Dependent on variety
✱	**Preferred conditions**	Sun
✱	**Origin**	China
✱	**Toxicity**	No reported toxicity

How to spot • Bamboo is quite untypical of traditional British garden plants, but familiar to many because it is so distinctive. Plants have tall, woody, hollow stems, usually greenish-yellow in colour. There are over 1,000 different varieties of bamboo, so leaf shape and ultimate height differ widely. Bamboo is technically a grass, but is grown in shrub borders or to provide structure and screening in this country.

Perks • There are two types of bamboo: clumping and running varieties. The former (clumping) are generally seen as attractive garden plants and will not spread beyond their welcome. Clumping cultivars are excellent for quickly covering an unattractive fence or providing speedy shade.

  WHAT IS THAT PLANT?

Nick Fewings

Pitfalls • Running bamboo, on the other hand, can become quite a menace. This type spreads by rhizomes, so new shoots can pop up many metres away from the original parent plant, sneaking under fences, into lawns and breaking concrete paving slabs in the process. Some still like to use running bamboo for screening purposes, as it grows very quickly, but it is highly advisable to plant it within a physical barrier dug deep into the soil to contain the plant's spread.

Did you know? • Bamboo is one of the fastest-growing plants in the world. Because the plant evolved in dense forest conditions, it adapted to reach the sunlight above the tree canopy as quickly as possible.

Blackthorn (*Prunus spinosa*)

✳	**Flowers**	March to May
✳	**Foliage**	Deciduous
✳	**Height**	7m
✳	**Spread**	4m
✳	**Preferred conditions**	Sun
✳	**Origin**	Europe
✳	**Toxicity**	Toxic to cats, dogs and horses
✳	**Also known as**	Buckthorn, skeg, sloe, sloe plum, snag

Merve Serhili Nasir

How to spot • This native bushy shrub or tree is found throughout the British countryside. It is one of the earliest shrubs to come into flower in spring, with creamy white blossoms appearing between March and May. Usually reaching about four metres, mature bushes grow into trees of up to seven metres. The branches, as the name suggests, are covered in spiky thorns. Leaves are oval and slightly crinkly around the edges. In the autumn, dark purplish-black berries – known as sloes – form on the branches. Long hedgerows of sloe bushes are frequently seen being rifled through by foragers – of both the human and animal variety – in the autumn.

Perks • This indigenous shrub is a major hit with wildlife – its early spring blooms provide nectar for bees. The rare black hairstreak butterfly also lays its eggs in blackthorn hedgerows. And for enthusiastic cooks (and drinkers), the fruit's potential for tipples and treats is a bonus.

Pitfalls • Blackthorn's, well, thorny nature makes it unsuitable for a garden where children play freely. The berries are also extremely unpleasant and sour if eaten raw.

Did you know? • The fruit of the blackthorn is used to make sloe gin, a sweet alcoholic liqueur, as well as jams and jellies. Wait until after the first frost to pick the berries: this splits their thick skins and allows the flavour to infuse better.

Boston ivy (*Parthenocissus tricuspidata*)

Author

✳	**Flowers**	July to September
✳	**Foliage**	Deciduous
✳	**Height**	20m
✳	**Spread**	8m
✳	**Preferred conditions**	Sun, partial shade, shade
✳	**Origin**	Asia
✳	**Toxicity**	No reported toxicity
✳	**Also known as**	Japanese creeper, Japanese ivy

How to spot • Boston ivy, like its lookalike Virginia creeper (p. 145), is often seen enveloping entire facades. But unlike Virginia creeper, Boston ivy (which actually originated in Japan, not the USA) has glossy green leaves with three tips rather than five. This difference can help you tell one from the other. Boston ivy has bluish berries, and unremarkable blossoms, but the late colour is the real attraction – look for a kaleidoscope of yellows, oranges and umbers as the plant nears its autumnal zenith.

Perks • As an option for covering walls, fences and other structures, Boston ivy is a more prudent option than a true ivy. It generally won't damage brickwork and its deciduous nature means it provides shade in summer but allows the warmth of winter sunlight to shine through in the darker, cooler months. Its foliage colour is a sight to behold, turning a slew of molten shades ending in an intense, deep red.

Pitfalls • A height of up to 20 metres? Clearly this isn't a plant that can grow just anywhere. It spreads both outwards and upwards, although it does take about a decade to reach its ultimate height. As the leaves fall in autumn, you'll be left with visibly bare stems over winter.

Did you know? • This woody vine is self-clinging, meaning it scales those walls of its own accord, using self-adhesive pads.

Buddleia (*Buddleia davidii*)

✳	**Flowers**	June to October
✳	**Foliage**	Semi-evergreen
✳	**Height**	4m
✳	**Spread**	8m
✳	**Preferred conditions**	Sun, dappled shade, partial shade
✳	**Origin**	China
✳	**Toxicity**	No reported toxicity
✳	**Also known as**	Butterfly bush, buddleja, summer lilac

Author

How to spot • When buddleia is in flower, you'll spot (and hear) its vibrant purple flower cones humming with bees and butterflies, a sight that gives this prolific shrub the nickname 'butterfly bush'. Its mostly evergreen foliage is a greyish-green with a slightly velvety texture, and the stems are woody with an arching appearance.

Perks • Its nectar draws in insects and its tall, arching stems provide shelter for birds, bats and even foxes. Compact cultivars are well suited to small spaces and can be grown in containers. And now many different varieties are available – from pure white to bi-coloured sherbet shades, all with that heady floral aroma.

Pitfalls • However, a word of warning: if the seed heads are left on the plant, they will likely disperse and spread widely. If you keep on top of the weeding, or don't mind the thought of a buddleia thicket in your patch, then no dice.

Did you know? • If you've ever sat on a train as it trundled along a British railway, you'll likely have passed swathes of buddleia, whether you were looking for it or not. It has spread widely along railway lines via windborne seeds, where it survives thanks to its ability to thrive in brick walls and masonry structures such as bridges.

Camellia (*Camellia* spp.)

Eleanor Burfitt

✳	Flowers	January to March
✳	Foliage	Evergreen
✳	Height	12m
✳	Spread	8m
✳	Preferred conditions	Dappled shade, partial shade
✳	Origin	Asia
✳	Toxicity	No reported toxicity

How to spot • Camellias can be small bushes, enormous shrubs, or anything in between. Their leaves are a very shiny dark green, shaped like ovals that thin to a narrow tip. Blowsy flowers can be pink, red or white or white and usually measure about 6–10cm in diameter. Camellias flower during the British winter, when little else is in bloom.

Eleanor Burfitt

Perks • In the right spot, elegant camellia flowers provide a welcome pop of colour in the winter months and evergreen foliage offers year-round interest.

Pitfalls • Camellias are not the easiest plants to care for: they're fussy about which soils they like (acidic, please!) and don't like too much sun, especially not in the morning after a frost.

Did you know? • White camellias play a starring role in Harper Lee's novel *To Kill a Mockingbird*, when Jem Finch plucks every last flower off a prejudiced neighbour's bush in a fit of rage.

Cape figwort (*Phygelius capensis*)

✳	**Flowers**	May to September
✳	**Foliage**	Semi-evergreen
✳	**Height**	1.5m
✳	**Spread**	1.5m
✳	**Preferred conditions**	Sun, dappled shade
✳	**Origin**	South Africa
✳	**Toxicity**	No reported toxicity
✳	**Also known as**	Cape fuchsia

Author

Author

How to spot • Take a moment to sit and observe the shrub you suspect is cape figwort. Do the tubular, orange flowers hang like bells from its stems? Are the leaves glossy and dark green, similar to a fuchsia? Peek inside a flower – it should have a yellow centre and display a more vivid colour on the inside. The mature plant forms a large, wide bush.

Perks • The drooping, bell-shaped blossoms of cape figwort are reason enough to grow it – so it's a bonus they continue to bloom over many months. A beautiful coral reddish-orange, the flowers hang from the foliage like many pairs of earrings, often swaying lightly in the wind.

Pitfalls • Averse to wet clay as well as cool climates, cape figwort needs warmth and sun to survive as a shrub. In most of the UK, it has been treated more like a herbaceous perennial – dying back over winter – but as our summers and winters see the mercury rise, its woody stems are frequently persisting through winter in mild regions.

Did you know? • Cape figwort belongs to the *Scrophulariaceae* plant family (try saying that three times fast) – the same one as our common flowers snapdragons (p. 90) and penstemon (p. 42). Examine the flowers closely and you may see the family resemblance.

Castor oil plant (*Fatsia japonica*)

✳	**Flowers**	October to November
✳	**Foliage**	Evergreen
✳	**Height**	4m
✳	**Spread**	4m
✳	**Preferred conditions**	Dappled shade, partial shade, full shade
✳	**Origin**	Asia
✳	**Toxicity**	No reported toxicity
✳	**Also known as**	Fig-leaf palm, glossy-leaved palm, Japanese aralia, paperplant, umbrella plant

How to spot • *Fatsia japonica* has become fashionable in recent years, often used in urban parks and municipal plantings. You're likely to find it growing best in partial or full shade. This evergreen plant has large, glossy, star-shaped leaves, and umbels of creamy white flowers in the autumn. These are followed by spheres of black fruit.

Perks • With a modern, tropical vibe, the castor oil plant might not be the choice of traditional cottage gardeners, but it can provide useful height at the back of a shady border and its intriguing leaf shape provides year-round visual interest. It is easy to look after among shrubs and exceptionally forgiving of neglect. Blackbirds, in particular, enjoy feasting on its berries.

Pitfalls • This plant definitely prefers the shade – you may notice its leaves turning yellow if it has been planted in full sun.

Did you know? • Because this plant doesn't mind low light levels, it's often sold as a house plant.

Author

Clematis (*Clematis montana, Clematis* spp.)

Author

✳	**Flowers**	Dependent on variety
✳	**Foliage**	Deciduous
✳	**Height**	12m
✳	**Spread**	4m
✳	**Preferred conditions**	Sun, dappled shade, partial shade
✳	**Origin**	Asia
✳	**Toxicity**	Toxic to humans, cats, dogs and horses
✳	**Also known as**	Himalayan clematis, mountain clematis

Oliver Ash

How to spot • These climbing vines are British favourites and come in all types of colours and sizes. *Clematis montana* is one of the most common garden varieties, often seen clothing a wall or shed. This eager climber produces masses of pale pink or white flowers in April and May beneath its tangle of intertwined stems. Flower size varies depending on the cultivar, but blooms tend to be saucer-shaped and pink or white.

Perks • Clematis montana are vigorous, floriferous plants in conditions they're happy with. They make great cover for fences and provide shelter for birds and insects.

Pitfalls • If the clematis you've identified isn't flowering much, it may need time to mature, or it may have been pruned incorrectly. The leaves can also develop powdery mildew later in the season. And clematis montana's rampant spread has been known to fell fences when left unchecked – so prudent positioning and pruning is probably wise!

Did you know? • The native wild form of clematis (*Clematis vitalba*) is known as Old Man's Beard and produces giant fluffy clouds of seed heads.

Dogwood (*Cornus sanguinea*)

Author

Andreas Rockstein

✳ **Flowers**	May to July	
✳ **Foliage**	Deciduous	
✳ **Height**	3m	
✳ **Spread**	2.5m	
✳ **Preferred conditions**	Sun, partial shade	
✳ **Origin**	Europe, Asia, North America	
✳ **Toxicity**	No reported toxicity	
✳ **Also known as**	Bloody dogwood, blood twig, catteridge tree, common cornel, dog cherry, dog tree, dogberry	

How to spot • This tree-like shrub is widespread across southern England, particularly in hedgerows and wooded areas. Dogwood leaves are smooth and green, with distinctly curved veins on the upper surface. In summer, creamy white flowers appear, turning to dark, purple–black fruits by autumn. When in bloom, you may be able to identify it from the foul smell given off by its flowers. In winter, the shiny red appearance of the new stems is very noticeable.

Perks • Other forms of dogwood are grown for their colourful stems in winter, and common dogwood offers the same benefit. Meanwhile, small mammals and birds enjoy feasting on the autumn berries.

Pitfalls • They do tend to self-seed, even in lawns they overhang, so you may find yourself pulling tiny trees up quite often once established.

Did you know? • The timber of dogwood is so strong that it was historically used to make arrows, herding poles and crucifixes.

Elder (*Sambucus nigra*)

✳ **Flowers**	May to July
✳ **Foliage**	Deciduous
✳ **Height**	10m
✳ **Spread**	4m
✳ **Preferred conditions**	Full sun, dappled shade, partial shade
✳ **Origin**	Europe, Asia
✳ **Toxicity**	Toxic to humans, cats, dogs and horses
✳ **Also known as**	Elderberry, European elder

Author

How to spot • In May and June you'll recognise the elder from the scent of its cream flowers – summery, sweet and aromatic. These grow in starry clusters and the fragrance will be familiar if you've ever enjoyed a glass of elderflower cordial. The leaves of the elder bush have a subtly serrated edge and are found in clusters of five or seven leaves.

Perks • The bushes can be short-lived but do grow fast, useful if you want to fill a space quickly. Discovering an elder tree is a plus for would-be foragers too – providing both elderflower blossom and berries. Birds and mice enjoy the berries, while many moth caterpillars rely on the foliage for sustenance.

Pitfalls • Another extraordinarily common plant that is unfortunately poisonous to us and our domesticated animals. While the blossoms are, of course, the source of cordial and wine, the roots, stems, seeds and leaves all produce toxic cyanide in the human body if ingested (though cooking the berries destroys the seeds' dangerous compounds). The smell of the blossoms is also rather divisive.

Did you know? • The *nigra* in the plant's botanical title refers to the black berries; however you can also find cultivated varieties with dark maroon leaves and lilac blossom.

Fig (*Ficus carica*)

Delia Giandeini

✳	**Flowers**	March to April
✳	**Foliage**	Deciduous
✳	**Height**	4m
✳	**Spread**	4m
✳	**Preferred conditions**	Sun
✳	**Origin**	Asia
✳	**Toxicity**	Toxic to humans, cats and dogs
✳	**Also known as**	Brown turkey fig, common fig

How to spot • A mature fig tree is hard to miss – unless their roots are contained, adult fig trees will grow to heights of 3–4m over a few decades, sprawling leisurely across a wall or fence. Figs can be bushy or more tree-like, and have distinctive leaves – with a glossy, leather-like appearance and distinct lobes. Each leaf measures 10–25cm and has clear white veins running between each lobe. The bark of a fig tree is light in colour and smooth. Green fruits, which ripen to purple, appear in spring, and are followed by a second crop later in the year, although this is unlikely to ripen in the UK climate.

Perks • Fresh, ripe figs are a luxury, expensive to buy, and so if you're a fan and have a fig tree growing in a sunny, sheltered spot, get feasting. The interesting foliage, although deciduous, is attractive and unusual among shrubs in this country.

Pitfalls • The fig is a tree that fares best in warm, Mediterranean-style climates, so is unlikely to thrive in a chilly location or frost pocket. And it is prone to running rampant: unless a tree's roots are restricted, the tree will produce more foliage than fig, and grow to heights that might irritate the nextdoor neighbours. It's also worth knowing that the sap of fig trees can trigger severe skin inflammation in susceptible people, cats and dogs.

Did you know? • The common fig is one of the oldest-known trees cultivated by man.

Flowering currant (*Ribes sanguineum*)

Judy Dean

* Flowers	April to May
* Foliage	Deciduous
* Height	2.5m
* Spread	1.2m
* Preferred conditions	Sun, dappled shade, partial shade
* Origin	North America
* Toxicity	No reported toxicity
* Also known as	Blood currant, pink-flowering currant, redflower currant

How to spot • Easiest to identify during its spring flowering period, the cerise blossoms hang from its branches like costume jewellery, drawing in ardent spectators and bees alike. The leaves resemble those of other currant bushes, so if you're familiar with gooseberry, blackcurrant or redcurrant foliage, you may recognise the similarities – mid-green, hand-shaped, with a sweet curranty smell when rubbed.

Perks • As a medium-sized shrub, flowering currant is large enough to make an impact but not so gigantic to look out of place in all but the smallest gardens. And it's happy in various conditions and soil types. The mid-spring blossoms are such a glowing hot pink that truly catch the eye.

Pitfalls • Incorrect pruning can avert flowering, as the blossoms are formed on buds grown in the previous season. And although its autumn fruits are edible they're not anything to write home about.

Did you know? • The classic British soft drink Ribena, flavoured with currants, takes its name from the plant genus – *Ribes*.

Forsythia (*Forsythia* spp.)

* Flowers	February to April
* Foliage	Deciduous
* Height	2m
* Spread	4m
* Preferred conditions	Sun, dappled shade
* Origin	Asia
* Toxicity	No reported toxicity
* Also known as	Golden bell

Author

How to spot • This is a plant best identified when in bloom. Forsythia's bright yellow flowers appear on bare branches, their vivid topaz contrasting with the dark bark of the plant's woody stems. After the flowers, the plant has dark green, oval leaves with smooth edges, which persist well into autumn.

Perks • These fast-growing shrubs can provide useful screening in a relatively short time. If you're responsible for a forsythia, read up on pruning to make the most of the flowers – which is the real reason to grow forsythia. The shrub offers little interest to humans the rest of year, but it more than makes up for this with its vivid spring showing.

Pitfalls • Or does it? Some would argue that – given the space it takes up and its uninteresting foliage – forsythia isn't worth its place in the garden. Birds can also feast on the buds, inhibiting the flowering.

Did you know? • Named Forsyth? You share a surname with the botanist who gave his name to the flower after discovering it in China – William Forsyth (1737–1804).

Hardy fuchsia (*Fuchsia magellanica*)

Author

*	**Flowers**	July to November
*	**Foliage**	Deciduous or semi-evergreen
*	**Height**	2.5m
*	**Spread**	1.5m
*	**Preferred conditions**	Dappled shade, partial shade, shade
*	**Origin**	South America, Oceania
*	**Toxicity**	No reported toxicity
*	**Also known as**	Lady's eardrops

How to spot • A fuchsia flower resembles a Borrower-sized ballet dancer wearing a tutu. Or perhaps a pair of dangly earrings (they're nicknamed lady's eardrops for a reason). Hardy fuchsias are shrubby and have dark green, oval leaves. The bauble-like flowers consist of a central tube ringed by five petals that form an upper cap. The flowers can be pink, purple, red, white – or, quite often, a combination.

Perks • Hardy fuchsias need little care to thrive and are reliable shrubs in all but the coldest regions. Aside from a few select varieties, these shrubs rarely grow too large and have a long flowering period. And those blooms are delicate (and edible!), with a slightly tropical air, brightening up dark corners.

Pitfalls • Caterpillars can take a liking to the foliage, feasting on the leaves. Fuchsia rust and grey mould, the latter causing tissue decay, can be an issue.

Did you know? • Tender fuchsias are broadly available in garden centres in the spring, with hundreds of varieties on offer in many colours. These are excellent as bedding plants or in hanging baskets, but won't survive the winter.

Hawthorn (*Crataegus monogyna*)

Author

✳	**Flowers**	May to June
✳	**Foliage**	Deciduous
✳	**Height**	15m
✳	**Spread**	8m
✳	**Preferred conditions**	Sun, partial shade
✳	**Origin**	Europe, Asia, North Africa
✳	**Toxicity**	No reported toxicity
✳	**Also known as**	May tree, one-seed hawthorn, quickthorn, whitehorn

How to spot • Look for hawthorn in May, when it's particularly noticeable thanks to its creamy blossoms. Red fruits produced in autumn – called 'haws' – are also a good marker for identification. These appear in autumn and winter. The leaves are glossy and separated into between three and seven pairs of lobes.

Perks • Unless it has outgrown its space, hawthorn is a beneficial addition to an outdoor space – it provides a habitat for all kinds of wildlife, from insects to rodents to birds. In fact, the flowers have adapted over the centuries to attract as many pollinators as possible. The pearly May blossoms are also a cultural indicator that spring has arrived.

Pitfalls • As its name declares, the tree's branches are covered in prickly spines, so wear gloves if pruning and keep young children out of harm's way. The smell of hawthorn blossom is also divisive. While it has a certain (slightly cloying) sweetness, it also contains the same chemical found in decaying flesh – adding an undeniable rotting smell to the plant's aromatic signature.

Did you know? • The hawthorn has a muddy history in Britain given its historic use as a hedging plant used to divide fields and keep the poor off private land. Even today, any long straight hedge that acts as a boundary between fields is almost certainly mostly hawthorn.

Hazel (*Corylus avellana*)

Author

✴ **Flowers**	February to March
✴ **Foliage**	Deciduous
✴ **Height**	8m
✴ **Spread**	8m
✴ **Preferred conditions**	Sun, partial shade
✴ **Origin**	Asia, Europe
✴ **Toxicity**	No reported toxicity
✴ **Also known as**	Cobnut, common filbert, European hazelnut, hale nut, hazelnut, stock nut, wood nut

How to spot • Hazel trees are common across the UK, often found in hedgerows, woodland and countryside gardens. Identify them in late winter and early spring by their yellow catkins, which arrive ahead of the leaves and hang in delicate clusters. Leaves are green, hairy and oval-shaped, but turn yellow before dropping in the autumn, while fruits come in the form of edible nuts.

Perks • Hazel trees are incredibly long-lived and incredibly useful. Hazel sticks can be used to make garden structures or support climbing plants like peas. The nuts can be gathered in autumn for culinary use – or left to nourish the dormice and squirrels that are so fond of them. And the dainty catkins are a welcome sight in February.

Yoksel Zok

Pitfalls • For the sturdiest stems, hazel trees do benefit from being coppiced – the process of chopping the tree down to the ground – on a five- to ten-year cycle. Otherwise, the stems can become overcrowded and the nuts difficult to reach.

Did you know? • Until the early twentieth century, hazelnuts (known as cobnuts when cultivated) were farmed en masse in Kent for sale as food. Nowadays, however, most of Britain's hazelnuts are imported from abroad.

Holly (*Ilex aquifolium*)

Author

✳	**Flowers**	May
✳	**Foliage**	Evergreen
✳	**Height**	15m
✳	**Spread**	8m
✳	**Preferred conditions**	Sun, dappled shade, partial shade, full shade
✳	**Origin**	Europe, Asia, North Africa
✳	**Toxicity**	Toxic to humans, cats, dogs and horses
✳	**Also known as**	English holly

How to spot • This festive favourite is a slow-growing shrub or tree that can eventually reach up to 15m in ideal conditions. Holly has dark green, shiny leaves with prickly serrated edges. Individual holly leaves can be shaped differently on a single plant: the leaves become spiky as a reaction to over-inquisitive and hungry wildlife. The foliage remains green all year. White flowers, beloved by bees, appear around the end of May, followed by ruby red berries on male trees.

Perks • Holly provides leaf colour all year round thanks to its evergreen foliage. Use it in winter wreaths and appreciate its myriad benefits to wildlife, including providing berries for birds and nectar for bees.

Pitfalls • Famously prickly, handling holly leaves isn't for the (literally) thin-skinned. And although the leaves may make for festive decorations, the berries are poisonous to people and pets.

Did you know? • Holly trees have been known to live for up to 300 years. In British folklore holly was thought to offer protection from numerous unwanted plights, including bad luck and thunder.

Honeysuckle (*Lonicera periclymenum*)

Author

✳	**Flowers**	June to August
✳	**Foliage**	Deciduous
✳	**Height**	5m
✳	**Spread**	2.5m
✳	**Preferred conditions**	Sun, dappled shade
✳	**Origin**	Europe, Asia, North Africa
✳	**Toxicity**	Toxic to humans, cats, dogs, horses and livestock
✳	**Also known as**	Bearbind, eglantine, wild honeysuckle, woodbine

How to spot • This incredibly fragrant climbing plant can be found sprawling up trees, shrubs and fences in the wild and in gardens. Many other cultivars are also found in the UK. Honeysuckle has dark green oval leaves that grow in pairs very close to the stem. From June to August, unusual trumpet-shaped flowers in pale yellow and white appear, visited by many different pollinators. In autumn, red berries appear.

Perks • The scent of wild honeysuckle is an aromatic addition to any outdoor space. It's also a hit with a wide variety of wildlife: long-tongued bees, butterflies and moths delight in its scented flowers, its climbing tendrils provide shelter for birds, and its autumnal berries are enjoyed by both birds and squirrels.

Janeson Keely

Pitfalls • A pest called honeysuckle aphid can cause the plant serious grief, leading to deformed and curled leaves. Powdery mildew is another potential issue. And if the shrub is climbing among other trees, it can distort their branches.

Did you know? • Honeysuckle can be spotted in several of the designs of British textile artist William Morris (1834–96).

Hydrangea (*Hydrangea* spp.)

*	**Flowers**	July to October
*	**Foliage**	Deciduous
*	**Height**	2m
*	**Spread**	1.5m
*	**Preferred conditions**	Dappled shade, partial shade
*	**Origin**	Asia
*	**Toxicity**	Toxic to cats, dogs and horses
*	**Also known as**	Hortensia

Author

Lacecap hydrangea. Author

Mophead hydrangea. Author

How to spot • Although there are several varieties of hydrangea, mophead hydrangeas are the most popular and widespread across the UK. This shrub, which you'll find thriving in a partially shady location, has a rounded shape and large clusters of flower heads throughout late summer and autumn. The leaves are oval and take on a reddish tinge in late summer and autumn. Flower heads are the real draw, varying in colour from white to purple to pink to blue, depending on the soil type. The flower heads are round and made up of many small blossoms.

Perks • Appreciate hydrangeas for their mass of ball-shaped flowers, at a time when other flowers may have gone over in the border. They're also excellent for drying, and their skeletal outlines persist in the winter garden. There are so many varieties that there's something for everyone. Beyond the traditional mophead type, lacecap and paniculata varieties offer their own unique charms.

Pitfalls • If your hydrangea is in baking sun, it's unlikely to thrive – consider relocating to partial shade. Avoid dry spots too – all hydrangeas hate being thirsty.

Did you know? • The name hydrangea derives from Greek and translates as 'water vessel'. Although originally chosen to describe its shape, it's also fitting because all hydrangeas like a great deal of water.

Japanese maple (*Acer palmatum*)

Eleanor Burfitt

✳	**Flowers**	April to May
✳	**Foliage**	Deciduous
✳	**Height**	10m
✳	**Spread**	8m
✳	**Preferred conditions**	Partial shade, dappled shade, shade
✳	**Origin**	Asia
✳	**Toxicity**	Toxic to horses
✳	**Also known as**	Acers, palmate maple

How to spot • You are most likely to find Japanese maples in shady, sheltered spots. They are also common container plants. The leaf shape should aid identification: it has the classic maple leaf shape seen on the Canadian national flag and bottles of maple syrup. In autumn, look out for glowing foliage in fiery shades of red, yellow and orange. Although some varieties can reach heights of ten metres most are much smaller.

Perks • Japanese maples are prized for their richly coloured autumn foliage. Often expensive to buy and difficult to grow from seed, count yourself lucky if you've found one in your garden. As they are slow-growing trees, they're also ideal for smaller spaces.

Pitfalls • That same slow-and-steady tortoise-like tendency can be a negative if you're looking for plants that will fill a garden in a few years.

Did you know? • The *palmatum* in the botanical classification is a reference to the hand-like leaves that resemble an open palm.

Lavender (*Lavandula angustifolia* and *Lavandula intermedia*)

Dorné Marting

✳	**Flowers**	June to September
✳	**Foliage**	Evergreen
✳	**Height**	1m
✳	**Spread**	1.5m
✳	**Preferred conditions**	Sun
✳	**Origin**	the Mediterranean
✳	**Toxicity**	Toxic to cats, dogs and horses

How to spot • Perhaps the easiest way to identify lavender is by its aromatic smell, familiar to many of us from scented bubble baths and soaps. Silvery-green leaves give way to a mass of delicate purple flowers in midsummer. Follow the sound of visiting bumblebees on the flowers to hunt down this common garden shrub.

Perks • Lavender is a popular plant for good reason, prized for its flowers and its fragrance, as well as its benefits to wildlife. It can be used as a hedge or in a border, ornamental vegetable patch or wild plot. Nostalgic for many due to its familiarity, the flowers are attractive to bees and butterflies, and can be used in baking and cooking.

Eleanor Burfitt

Pitfalls • Lavender cannot be divided, and so without pruning it can outgrow its space or become overly woody. In shade, it will become leggy as its stems struggles towards the sun. And increasingly there is worry that a plant disease called *Xylella fastidiosa* will at some point arise in the UK and wreak havoc on this country's many lavenders, which are highly susceptible to the bacterium.

Did you know? • The name lavender comes from the Latin 'lavare', meaning to wash – the Romans, and later the Elizabethans, used lavender to perfume their clothes.

Lavender cotton (*Santolina chamaecyparissus*)

✳	**Flowers**	July to August
✳	**Foliage**	Evergreen
✳	**Height**	50cm
✳	**Spread**	1m
✳	**Preferred conditions**	Sun
✳	**Origin**	the Mediterranean
✳	**Toxicity**	No reported toxicity
✳	**Also known as**	Cotton lavender, ground cypress

Author

How to spot • Don't be fooled by the name – this Mediterranean plant is neither cotton nor lavender, although its silvery foliage could be said to mimic the latter. Lavender cotton has woolly, fragrant leaves that grow on silver branches and bright yellow, pom pom-like flowers that begin to bloom in July. It is usually planted in a sunny spot.

Perks • The plant is evergreen, so its silvery leaves provide welcome interest in a garden over the winter months. Its soft leaves are also perfect for a sensory or therapeutic garden like those sometimes located in hospitals, care homes and day centres.

Pitfalls • If unpruned, the shrub can begin to look slightly bedraggled – cut back straight after flowering to keep it looking neat and tidy.

Did you know? • Despite its Mediterranean roots, this plant is fully hardy and can weather UK frosts without dissent.

Lilac (*Syringa vulgaris*)

Author

✳	**Flowers**	May
✳	**Foliage**	Deciduous
✳	**Height**	5m
✳	**Spread**	4m
✳	**Preferred conditions**	Sun
✳	**Origin**	East Asia, south-eastern Europe
✳	**Toxicity**	No reported toxicity
✳	**Also known as**	Common lilac, pipe privet

How to spot • Lilacs are shrubs or multi-stemmed trees. The plant's leaves are simple and unexceptional, and fall in the autumn, so you'll find identification easiest during the flowering period in spring. Look out for the conical flowers' strong, sweet scent and the pale mauve that gives the colour lilac its name. White varieties of lilac are also available.

Perks • Lilacs are a common garden plant for good reason. Although their foliage isn't much to write home about, the heady perfume of lilac flowers heralds the arrival of spring and fills a gap in the flowering year, when spring bulbs may have gone over but roses are yet to bloom.

Pitfalls • The lilac's glorious, scented flowers are both its crowning glory and its drawback – they only stick around for a few short weeks a year in mid-spring.

Did you know? • The scent of lilac is strongest when the bushes are grown in bright, full sunlight. Purple varieties, as opposed to white, are the most fragrant.

Mahonia (*Mahonia* spp.)

Jean-Jacques Abalain

✷ **Flowers**	November to February
✷ **Foliage**	Evergreen
✷ **Height**	2–4m dependent on variety
✷ **Spread**	2–4m dependent on variety
✷ **Preferred conditions**	Sun, dappled shade, partial shade, shade
✷ **Origin**	Asia, North America
✷ **Toxicity**	No reported toxicity

How to spot • Look for shiny, dark green leaves with sharp, frilled edges – similar to holly foliage – and thicker woody stems at the base. From late autumn to late winter, the yellow pearls of flowers are difficult to miss – vivid in colour and humming with

Vall Ben

winter bumblebees, the best cultivars display many strands of small, butter-coloured flowers, draped over the foliage like necklaces. These have a mild but fragrant scent. The blossoms are followed by black berries.

Perks • Mahonia is a pretty utilitarian shrub – tolerant of shade, even under trees, green all year round, offering bright colour in winter when, arguably, we (and those winter bees) need it most.

Pitfalls • The leaves can be scorched by cold winds if planted in an exposed location. Most types of mahonia are fully hardy in the UK, but a handful don't cope so well with the cold, so it is worth trying to identify the variety you have growing.

Did you know? • Mahonia wood is the same radiant yellow as the flowers and can be used to make a similar-coloured dye.

Mexican orange blossom (*Choisya ternata*)

Bryony Bowie

✳	**Flowers**	April to May
✳	**Foliage**	Evergreen
✳	**Height**	2.5m
✳	**Spread**	2.5m
✳	**Preferred conditions**	Sun, dappled shade
✳	**Origin**	North America
✳	**Toxicity**	No reported toxicity
✳	**Also known as**	Choisya, Mexican orange plant, Mexican orange flower

How to spot • Mexican orange blossom is a very popular garden shrub for good reason, with glossy oval leaves and fragrant flowers. Foliage can be green, lime or yellow with each leaf divided into three leaflets. The sweet-smelling clusters of flowers are cream in colour, visited by honeybees, and generally appear from late April to May, although this depends on the variety.

Perks • *Choisya* are one of the most dependable shrubs grown in the UK, flowering year after year, and hardy down to -10°C. Blossoms can even appear sporadically in the winter months – I've gleefully, gratefully noted one particular specimen in Oxford

Dawn Woolcott

blooming its heart out in January. Their hardworking foliage is evergreen, too – a real bonus in winter, providing continuous green and interest in a border.

Pitfalls • Very young plants, which will be small, are attractive to slugs and snails and can suffer damage from which they will not recover. However, once the shrubs bed in properly, few pests or diseases can hurt them.

Did you know? • The plant's name was chosen in honour of Swiss botanist Jacques Choisy (1799–1859).

Mock orange (*Philadelphus* spp.)

✳	**Flowers**	May to July
✳	**Foliage**	Deciduous
✳	**Height**	2.5m
✳	**Spread**	2.5m
✳	**Preferred conditions**	Sun, partial shade
✳	**Origin**	Asia, North America
✳	**Toxicity**	No reported toxicity
✳	**Also known as**	Philadelphus

Author

How to spot • This is a plant best identified with your nose – although you only have a short window in early summer to do so. The shrub has an orange blossom fragrance that comes from the plant's profusion of cup-shaped white flowers. Woody stems have an arching habit. The plant is deciduous, so will lose its leaves in autumn.

Perks • The heady aroma of mock orange is one that – once smelled – is hard to deny yourself. The shrub will tolerate all but the wettest soils and live for many years. And the vision of it garlanded in white lacy blossom, like a bride at the altar, is a sight to behold.

Pitfalls • Pruning can be tricky to get your head around, and if carried out incorrectly can compromise flowering. Mock oranges aren't in flower for long, but I'm of the opinion that their potent fragrance – often smelled from several metres away – is more than worth it.

Did you know? • A variety of *Philadelphus* is the official flower of the US state of Idaho.

Pampas grass (*Cortaderia selloana*)

✳	**Flowers**	July to October
✳	**Foliage**	Evergreen
✳	**Height**	4m
✳	**Spread**	2.5m
✳	**Preferred conditions**	Sun
✳	**Origin**	South America
✳	**Toxicity**	No reported toxicity

Harry Rose

How to spot • Pampas is a common sight in front gardens, still – a hangover from the 1970s, when this tall, tufted grass was extremely popular. Evergreen and clump-forming, the plant has green grass-like leaves with a blue tint and upright stems topped with fuzzy, cloud-like tufts of beige. It stands tall and upright – its size making it pretty hard to miss.

Perks • Size alone means this grass makes a statement. And after several decades relegated to the sin bin, it's coming back into fashion in line with the resurgence of grasses and renewed interest in dried floral arrangements.

Pitfalls • The grass has a slightly sordid reputation – legend (now discredited) has it that its presence outside a residence in the latter half of the twentieth century was evidence of a household open to partner swapping. In the western USA and New Zealand, pampas grass has become invasive but that's unlikely to become a problem in the UK unless the climate warms significantly.

Did you know? • The leaves are razor sharp at the edges, so handle with care.

Passion flower (*Passiflora* spp.)

Author

✳	**Flowers**	July to October
✳	**Foliage**	Semi-evergreen
✳	**Height**	12m
✳	**Spread**	4m
✳	**Preferred conditions**	Sun, dappled shade
✳	**Origin**	South America
✳	**Toxicity**	Toxic to humans, cats, dogs and horses
✳	**Also known as**	Apricot vine, granadilla, maypop, passion vine

How to spot • You're most likely to find passion flower vines covering a wall or fence, particularly a south-facing one – this tropical vine loves the sun. The leaves are usually at least partly evergreen, so you may be able to identify this climber year round. From July to mid-autumn, broad, saucer-like flowers appear. These normally have white petals with bright blue and purple filaments extending from the centre. In autumn, small orange fruits form.

Perks • In a sunny position, a passion flower makes a bold and unusual statement and can be a beautiful and rapid way to cover a fence. The otherworldly flowers are unique among flowers commonly found in Britain, with a faintly extraterrestrial aura. And the leaves are a pleasing shape too, pointed with three to five lobes like a child learning to count using their fingers.

Pitfalls • Passion flower's meridional origins mean it enjoys a good bake in the sun – consider moving if you find one in shade, where it will not thrive. The fruits are edible, but are not particularly tasty! And be careful, the roots and leaves are poisonous.

Did you know? • The passion flower has strong associations with Christianity. The flower's corona is used as a symbol for Jesus' thorn of crowns.

Perennial sweet pea (*Lathyrus latifolius*)

✳	**Flowers**	June to September
✳	**Foliage**	Deciduous
✳	**Height**	3m
✳	**Spread**	1m
✳	**Preferred conditions**	Sun, partial shade
✳	**Origin**	Europe, North Africa
✳	**Toxicity**	Toxic to humans, cats, dogs and horses
✳	**Also known as**	Broad-leaved sweet pea, everlasting sweet pea, perennial peavine

How to spot • The everlasting sweet pea, as it is also known, looks very similar to the annual sweet peas grown every year by millions of home gardeners and allotment holders. It has climbing tendrils and long, fragile stems. By midsummer, you'll notice a profusion of pinkish-purple, pea-like flowers. Seed pods look very similar to edible peas.

Perks • Unlike its annual relative, the perennial version has the benefit of returning year on year, so there's no need to remember to sow seeds each autumn or spring. And scented or not, the cerise flowers are undoubtedly eye-catching, and the climbing tendrils can quickly cover a fence.

Author

Rose of Sharon (*Hibiscus syriacus*)

✳	**Flowers**	July to September
✳	**Foliage**	Deciduous
✳	**Height**	2.5m
✳	**Spread**	2m
✳	**Preferred conditions**	Sun
✳	**Origin**	Asia
✳	**Toxicity**	No reported toxicity
✳	**Also known as**	Korean rose, rose mallow, shrub althaea, tree hollyhock

Author

How to spot • Rose of Sharon is a hardy shrub that grows in the shape of a vase, thinner at the base and wider at the top. The saucer-like flowers look similar to hollyhocks (p. 77) and have very visible stamens at their centre. The blooms have five petals and come in various shades of purple, pink, white, red and blue, occasionally with a ring of a different colour surrounding the stamen surrounding the stamen. The green–yellow leaves sport visible veins.

Perks • This showy hibiscus can look quite remarkable, especially in the built-up suburbs where it is a common sight in front gardens. The array of colours available and how easy it is to care for have made it a firm favourite in Britain.

Pitfalls • Despite its charms, the shrub is a case of 'not much to see here' for much of the year. The leaves do not turn a beautiful, bright shade in the autumn and often take a long time to appear in the spring.

Did you know? • *Hibiscus syriacus* is the national flower of South Korea, depicted on banknotes and the presidential seal.

Rosemary (*Salvia rosmarinus*)

Paul Hanaoka

✳ Flowers	March to May	
✳ Foliage	Evergreen	
✳ Height	2.5m	
✳ Spread	2.5m	
✳ Preferred conditions	Sun	
✳ Origin	the Mediterranean	
✳ Toxicity	No reported toxicity	
✳ Also known as	Old man, rose of the sea, southernwood	

How to spot • Rosemary will already be familiar to most via the supermarket or the dinner table, even if you don't count yourself as particularly interested in plants. The plant is a bushy and upright shrub, richly scented, with leather-like deep green needles that horizontally adorn its stems. Beginning in March – or sometimes before – the shrub bursts into bloom with small, blue–purple flowers festooned along its stems.

Perks • That scent! Those periwinkle-coloured flowers! As well as providing a year-round supply of the herb to cook with, rosemary blossoms provide early-spring riches for the bees.

Evergreen leaves ensure interest throughout the year. Easy to care for and happy in a big, well-drained pot, this herb is simple and delightfully fragrant – even just touching the plant as you pass it releases the oils in the leaves that give it that redolent scent.

Pitfalls • If planted anywhere but full sun, rosemary will grow leggy as it strives to reach the light. It can also grow woody and outsized if not pruned regularly after flowering. And thanks to its balmy Mediterranean origins, rosemary isn't fully protected from frost. The UK's mild climate means losing shrubs is rare, but severe frosts can kill off plants entirely.

Did you know? • In 2019, rosemary's Latin botanical name was changed from *Rosmarinus officinalis* to *Salvia officinalis*, as improved research methods revealed it is not its own species but part of the sage (*Salvia*) genus.

Author

Smoke bush (*Cotinus coggygria*)

✳	**Flowers**	June to July
✳	**Foliage**	Deciduous
✳	**Height**	4m
✳	**Spread**	4m
✳	**Preferred conditions**	Sun, partial shade
✳	**Origin**	Europe, Asia
✳	**Toxicity**	No reported toxicity
✳	**Also known as**	Smoke tree

How to spot • Deep, vivid colours set this shrub apart: look for rounded, plum-coloured or green leaves from spring to autumn and masses of pink feathery plumes in summer. The flowers that do make it to the fruit stage are small and green, but are generally dwarfed by those fluffy masses that turn from pink to deep purple as the season progresses.

Perks • Purple-leaved smoke bushes offer vibrant colour for much of the year and their diaphanous pink clouds of flowers are truly a sight to behold.

Pitfalls • Smoke bushes can grow to 4m in height and 4m wide, so large varieties in smaller spaces may need to be reined in with judicious pruning. If you're planting one yourself, smaller cultivars are also available.

Did you know? • The smoke bush is a close relation of the plant that provides the spice sumac, frequently used in Middle Eastern cooking.

Author

Star jasmine (*Trachelospermum jasminoides*)

Liz West

Helena Munoz

✳	**Flowers**	June to August
✳	**Foliage**	Evergreen
✳	**Height**	8m
✳	**Spread**	8m
✳	**Preferred conditions**	Sun, dappled shade, partial shade
✳	**Origin**	Asia
✳	**Toxicity**	No reported toxicity
✳	**Also known as**	Chinese ivy, Chinese jasmine, trader's jasmine

How to spot • Don't be fooled by the name – star jasmine isn't actually a type of jasmine. It got its name because the intense fragrance emitted by its creamy white, star-shaped flowers is said to be similar to jasmine. A woody climbing vine, it will often scramble up fences or trellises. The flowers have five petals and bloom from June to August, while leaves, green all year, turn reddish in the autumn.

Perks • Fast-growing, fragrant, versatile – star jasmine is a popular choice for a hedge or fence cover for a reason. The evergreen leaves turn a lovely bronze shade in the autumn, and the flowers are very attractive to bees.

Pitfalls • Spreading to heights and widths of eight metres star jasmine needs to be sited carefully and have a sturdy trellis or support on which to grow. It will also fail to thrive in an exposed, cold location.

Did you know? • The plant is sometimes still known as confederate jasmine. This is thought to relate to the confederacy of Malaysia.

Virginia creeper (*Parthenocissus quinquefolia*)

✶	**Flowers**	June to July
✶	**Foliage**	Deciduous
✶	**Height**	20m
✶	**Spread**	8m
✶	**Preferred conditions**	Sun, partial shade
✶	**Origin**	North America
✶	**Toxicity**	Toxic to humans, cats, dogs and horses
		American ivy, false grape, five-finger, five-leaved ivy, wild wood vine, woodbine, Victoria creeper

How to spot • Virginia creeper is a fast-growing, woody vine that climbs and climbs – it's been reported to reach heights of 20 metres. It can be identified by its distinctive leaves, which are hand-shaped and have five leaflets. Also look out for the manner of its ascent – it doesn't need tying in, as it attaches itself to walls and fences with tiny sticky discs, similar to the way lizards use suction pads on their feet to climb vertically. In autumn, Virginia creeper is difficult to miss, given its vibrant red foliage and black berries.

Perks • Despite its less-than-charming reputation, Virginia creeper is a feature of many gardens, favoured for its vivid autumn colour. Its extreme height means it can be used to cloak walls of buildings, although that of course makes it less suitable for smaller gardens. *Anne Nygård*

Pitfalls • There's no law against planting or nurturing Virginia creeper on your patch, but the plant is listed on Schedule 9 of the UK Wildlife & Countryside Act. This means that while its cultivation is permitted in your own garden, you must take appropriate action to stop its spread beyond.

Did you know? • Red Virginia creeper is both the subject and title of a painting by Edvard Munch (1864–1944).

Wisteria (*Wisteria* spp.)

✳	**Flowers**	May to June
✳	**Foliage**	Deciduous
✳	**Height**	10m
✳	**Spread**	20m
✳	**Preferred conditions**	Sun, dappled shade
✳	**Origin**	North America, Asia
✳	**Toxicity**	Toxic to humans, cats, dogs and horses

Annie Spratt

How to spot • Hunting down wisteria has become something of a cult in recent years, with members gracing social media sites with images of its cascading, unforgettably purple flowers. Its sheer height and spread make it hard to miss. Often seen clothing the walls of houses or trailing over trellises and pergolas, the woody vines and twining stems have narrow, pinnate leaves, normally pale green in colour. The flowers, which appear in spring and have a sweet, musky fragrance, are held in drooping clusters. They can be purple, pink or white – the lilac variety is most widespread.

WHAT IS THAT PLANT?

Perks • A wisteria in full bloom is a sight to behold, luminescently purple and humming with pollinators. The plant is an extraordinarily enthusiastic climber, making it perfect for covering buildings and other structures.

Pitfalls • Wisteria isn't the easiest plant to care for if you're new to gardening – it benefits from pruning twice a year and can fail to flower if this is done incorrectly. If planted in the shade, it will produce fewer flowers – and in deep shade, it won't flourish at all. Then there's the fact that young plants take seven years to mature; you won't get flowers before then.

Did you know? • Wisteria belongs to the pea family, which is why its flowers bear a resemblance to those of lupins (p. 39) and the perennial sweet pea (p. 137).

Annie Spratt

Witch hazel (*Hamamelis* spp.)

✳	**Flowers**	January to February
✳	**Foliage**	Deciduous
✳	**Height**	2.5m
✳	**Spread**	5m
✳	**Preferred conditions**	Sun, partial shade
✳	**Origin**	North America, Asia
✳	**Toxicity**	No reported toxicity
✳	**Also known as**	Wych hazel

Author

How to spot • Witch hazel – yes, the very same witch hazel mixed into teenage blemish potions – is easiest to spot in late winter when the yellow or orange flowers emit a spicy aroma. These citrus-coloured blossoms look just like the orange or lemon zest that collects beneath your grater in the kitchen. They have four petals and appear before the branches come into leaf.

Perks • Witch hazel is pretty self-sufficient and low maintenance, needing little pruning and with flowers resistant to frost. The fact that it blooms in winter is a virtue too, providing scent and beauty in a barren season.

Pitfalls • If patience isn't your particular virtue, know that witch hazel is slow-growing, taking about two decades to reach its ultimate height.

Did you know? • Although its name suggests magical connotations, the 'witch' in its title actually comes from the Anglo-Saxon word 'wych', meaning 'to bend' – denoting its bandy stems.

Weeds & wildflowers

What is a weed? It's an age-old question, one even famous writers have turned their pens to. American writer Ralph Waldo Emerson famously pondered the definition of a weed, wondering if it was in fact just a plant whose virtues had not yet been acknowledged. Others might disagree, categorising a weed as an unwanted invader – something to curse at, douse with chemicals, or to dig up at first glance.

I've often found applying this kind of morality to plants a curious phenomenon, even as I sometimes fall into it myself. In blaming nature, we are surely pointing the finger at the wrong culprit. Humans were the ones who dreamt up the concept of weeds. And people were the ones who transported plants around the world, introducing 'non-native' species that became 'invasive'. What's more, most modern plants we know as weeds evolved with the advent of agriculture as we now know it, thriving on soil that had been disturbed – yet more evidence that people, not the plants, are the real issue.

I tend to subscribe to the following school of thought (itself far from original): weeds are a construct invented by humans, rather than a strict botanical classification. Any plant growing where it is not wanted could be considered a weed, or perhaps a wildflower when found outside cultivated land. Tomato seedlings, for example, often pop up in borders where gardeners have spread homemade compost. These are treated as weeds and deftly pulled out by hand, while in the veg patch, the very same gardener will happily feed them a weekly dose of tomato fertiliser and look forward to their juicy fruits.

In years past, amateur gardeners might have spent their Sunday afternoons pouring boiling water on dandelion heads or applying pesticide to the tendrils of bindweed poking through nextdoor's fence. Thankfully, ideas about 'weeds' are in flux, and wildlife-friendly gardening movements aim to do away with the rigidity of categorising weeds previously seen, instead adopting a gentler approach. Leave the dandelions be, the bees love them, they say. Herb Robert (p. 182) is rather like a geranium if you squint. Perhaps mallow, too.

I chose to call this chapter weeds and wildflowers, and to group plants considered one or both together, because in many cases, weeds in the garden are just wild plants in the 'wrong' place. Weeds and wildflowers are united by a few attributes, too. They thrive on soil that has been dug over, can spread widely if left to their own devices, and are incredibly adaptable and abundant.

Of course, some weeds are awkward. I certainly curse the speedwells (p. 171) and bindweeds (p. 150) that are fond of my allotment soil, pretty though the flowers are. Giant hogweed (p. 173) poses a grave threat to human health, while the spread of Japanese knotweed (p. 187) is regulated by law. But that aside, the plants in this chapter are just that: plants. Weed them out, leave them be – use your judgement. Reconsidering the concept of a weed or wild plant can open our minds to new possibilities about gardening and quell the illusion that we have any sort of control over nature. I hope that you might be inspired to make room for some of the so-called weeds and wildflowers in your outdoor space after reading the chapter that follows.

Bindweed (*Calystegia sepium* and *Convolvulus arvensis*)

Author

✳	**Flowers**	June to September
✳	**Foliage**	Deciduous
✳	**Height**	3m
✳	**Spread**	2m
✳	**Preferred conditions**	Sun
✳	**Origin**	Europe
✳	**Toxicity**	Toxic to cats, dogs and horses
✳	**Also known as**	Bellbird, bearbind, corn bind, field bindweed, heavenly trumpets, hedge bindweed, wild morning glory

Author

How to spot • There are two types of bindweed, both common in British gardens: hedge bindweed (*Calystegia sepium*) and field bindweed (*Convolvulus arvensis*). They have similar characteristics: twirling, green, vine-like stems and trumpet-shaped flowers. Hedge bindweed is the larger of the pair; its heart-shaped leaves are about double the size of the field variety. It has large, white flowers and is often seen scaling fences, railings and trees. Field bindweed has darker green leaves, which tend to sprawl across lawns and bare soil, and pink and white flowers with a subtle striped pattern.

Perks • Ironically, for a plant that is the source of much exasperation for so many gardeners, the flowers are pretty enough, with the candy-striped design of field bindweed blooms particularly so.

Pitfalls • Try as you might to cull it, bindweeds are difficult to fully eradicate, given their spreading roots. The roots of field bindweed (*Convolvulus arvensis*) grow the deepest, reaching up to six metres below the soil.

Did you know? • Field bindweed is one of the most troublesome agricultural weeds: it's a major blight on cereal crops as it impedes their growth.

Bramble (*Rubus fruticosus*)

Author

✳	**Flowers**	June to August
✳	**Foliage**	Deciduous
✳	**Height**	2.5m
✳	**Spread**	>8m
✳	**Preferred conditions**	Sun, dappled shade, partial shade
✳	**Origin**	Europe
✳	**Toxicity**	No reported toxicity
✳	**Also known as**	Blackberry, wild blackberry

How to spot • Look out for prickly stems with a long, arching appearance. Brambles can grow very tall – as anyone who's stood on tiptoes to nab a ripe blackberry out of reach will attest. The dark green leaves, which can survive the winter, have jagged edges and are usually seen in groups of three or five. Pink or white flowers, similar in appearance to wild roses but smaller in size, appear in midsummer, turning to juicy blackberries by August and into autumn.

Perks • While you might not willingly invite them into a well-kept garden border, they provide delicious berries and have benefits to wildlife – from birds to insects to mammals – and can either be trained or left to ramble in wilder patches. And then there's all the potential for crumble and preserves.

Pitfalls • Brambles can be tricky to remove once they have become established, as many a worn-out allotment holder will attest. Removing them is little fun either, thanks to the deep roots and spiny stems.

Did you know? • Brambles belong to the same plant family as roses, united by their barbed thorns. However, thornless cultivars are now available for keen blackberry growers.

Bristly oxtongue (*Helminthotheca echioides*)

Bryony Bowie

✳	**Flowers**	June to September
✳	**Foliage**	Deciduous
✳	**Height**	1m
✳	**Spread**	50cm
✳	**Preferred conditions**	Sun
✳	**Origin**	the Mediterranean
✳	**Toxicity**	No reported toxicity
✳	**Also known as**	Milton Keynes weed, oxtongue, prickly oxtongue

How to spot • The key to identifying this plant hides in its name: the oval leaves of bristly oxtongue, as the name suggests, have a stubbly, stiff, blistered texture. I can't look at the plant now without thinking of the rough, brush-like look of a cow's tongue. In well-maintained lawns, you're unlikely to spot it – this weed prefers bare earth and neglected turf. The dandelion-like flowers measure just twenty-five millimetres in diameter.

Perks • Moths and butterflies enjoy the flowers' nectar, but that's about where the benefits end – the prickly spines mean the leaves aren't very appetising to other wildlife.

Pitfalls • Stepping on a clump of bristly oxtongue is a rather unpleasant experience, given its scratchy texture. And the weed has a deep root that can make it tricky to uproot.

Did you know? • One of the plant's common names is Milton Keynes weed, apparently because it is so often spotted in the Buckinghamshire town.

Chickweed (*Stellaria media*)

∗	Flowers	January to December
∗	Foliage	Semi-evergreen
∗	Height	50cm
∗	Spread	50cm
∗	Preferred conditions	Sun, dappled shade, partial shade
∗	Origin	Europe, Asia
∗	Toxicity	Toxic to humans and horses
∗	Also known as	Adder's mouth, chick wittles, mouse ear, satin flower, starweed, starwort, stitchwort, passerina, tongue grass, white bird's eye, winter weed

How to spot • Chickweed is an extremely common weed throughout the UK, even as far north as Shetland. It prospers both on cultivated ground and neglected sites. It can be seen all year round in beds and borders, allotments and veg patches – anywhere there is bare soil for it to capitalise on. The plant is small, usually about 15 centimetres high, although it can reach 50 centimetres when in flower. A mass of roots sits at the centre of the plant, from which many branching, sprawling stems arise. The foliage is bright green, with endearingly small, rounded leaves that sit in pairs on either side of the stem. Tiny white flowers, most often seen in winter and spring, have five petals.

Author

Perks • The seeds on plants left behind provide a good source of food for small birds. And there's nothing particularly offensive about the starry white flowers.

Pitfalls • Chickweed spreads very quickly by seed, easily carried on the wind, in compost, on the soles of shoes – and each plant can produce five or six generations of seed each year. However, it's easy to pull out by hand.

Did you know? • The name chickweed comes from the fact that it was formerly fed to caged birds.

Cleavers (*Galium aparine*)

✱ **Flowers**	May to July
✱ **Foliage**	Deciduous
✱ **Height**	50cm
✱ **Spread**	1.5m
✱ **Preferred conditions**	Sun, dappled shade, partial shade, shade
✱ **Origin**	Europe, Asia, North America
✱ **Toxicity**	No reported toxicity
✱ **Also known as**	Bobby buttons, catchweed, claggy meggies, goosegrass, gollenweed, gripgrass, kisses, stickyweed, sticky willy, sweethearts, robin-run-the-hedge, Velcro plant

Bryony Bowie

How to spot • This is one of the easiest weeds to identify by touch – although gardening gloves are recommended! Also known as stickyweed, the plant is covered in fine hooked hairs that attach to other plants and human limbs whenever they get the chance. Some will know it as the 'Velcro plant' for this reason. It appears in early spring with asterisk-shaped leaves and long, creeping stems, and puts out tiny, white, star-shaped flowers from late spring.

Perks • The starry flowers have a certain appeal, especially when scaling trees in woodland.

Pitfalls • Cleavers plants spread widely by seed and are most often found on waste ground, but they can crowd out other plants if left to spread unchecked in gardens. It will also stick to your clothes, pets and anything else it comes into contact with. Some people can develop an itchy skin rash after touching the plant.

Did you know? • The roots of the plant have previously been used to make a red dye.

Couch grass (*Elymus repens*)

Visnu Deva

✴	**Flowers**	May to October
✴	**Foliage**	Deciduous
✴	**Height**	1m
✴	**Spread**	1m
✴	**Preferred conditions**	Sun
✴	**Origin**	Europe
✴	**Toxicity**	No reported toxicity
✴	**Also known as**	Common couch, quack grass, quick grass, scutch, twitch grass, wickens

How to spot • Couch, or twitch, grass is a very widespread grass generally thought of as a weed in this country. It has wiry, thick, green stalks that grow in tufts and produces small rows of beige flower heads in the summer. The edges of the leaves can be sharp, and are shaped like blades. It is extremely common in gardens and on allotments.

Pitfalls • Like many weeds, couch grass loves cultivated land – so digging it up tends to only hasten its spread. It can even regrow from minuscule pieces of root left behind.

It mainly reproduces via sneaky underground stems and can easily head into flower beds from a neighbouring lawn.

Did you know? • Despite the bad press common couch gets these days, it served a useful purpose in the Second World War. Its roots contain substances that help to rid excess salt and water from the body, reducing blood pressure in the process, and so the plant was collected and dispensed for this purpose when medicines ran short in wartime.

Cow parsley (*Anthriscus sylvestris*)

Author

✳	**Flowers**	April to June
✳	**Foliage**	Deciduous
✳	**Height**	1.5m
✳	**Spread**	30cm
✳	**Preferred conditions**	Sun, dappled shade, partial shade
✳	**Origin**	Europe, Asia, northern Africa
✳	**Toxicity**	No reported toxicity
✳	**Also known as**	Fairy lace, Grandpa's pepper, hedge parsley, kex, lady's lace, mother die, rabbit meat, Queen Anne's lace, Spanish lace, wild chervil

How to spot • For a few weeks each May, my home county – and much of the English countryside – is marked by rising constellation-like spires of cow parsley, their frothy white umbels dancing in the newly golden evening light. This wild herb is often seen on roadsides, in hedgerows and on the edges of meadows and woodlands. It has green, fern-like foliage (like carrot or edible parsley leaves) and umbels of frothy white flowers. Cow parsley is one of the earliest umbellifers to come into flower, which may help you to distinguish it from later-flowering umbellifers like wild carrot (*Daucus carota*) and wild angelica (*Angelica sylvestris*).

Perks • Cow parsley is a boon for bees and hoverflies and looks quite similar to more heavily marketed lace-like flowers like bishop's flower (*Ammi majus*) and garden angelica (*Angelica archangelica*). It has a floaty, ethereal appearance that is very much on trend.

Pitfalls • If growing in a border or vegetable plot, cow parsley can spread rampantly so consider your options if the spot is already earmarked for something else. It also looks very similar to some of our most toxic plants, like hemlock (although without its purple-marked stem), so it is best to handle with caution and be absolutely sure your identification is correct.

Did you know? • The common name for cow parsley (and wild carrot, p. 213) is Queen Anne's lace, but the origins of this are somewhat hazy. Some say the name is the result of a legend that these flowers would bloom for Queen Anne, who often travelled in May, mimicking the delicate lace fashions popular with royals of the day. Others believe it refers to Queen Anne's hobby of lace-making. But nobody can agree on which Queen Anne!

Creeping wood sorrel (*Oxalis corniculata*)

✱	**Flowers**	May to September
✱	**Foliage**	Deciduous
✱	**Height**	20cm
✱	**Spread**	20cm
✱	**Preferred conditions**	Sun
✱	**Origin**	Europe, Asia
✱	**Toxicity**	No reported toxicity
✱	**Also known as**	Greenhouse weed, procumbent wood sorrel, sleeping beauty

Author

How to spot • This small, low-growing plant is incredibly common in gardens of all situations and sizes, displaying a special soft spot for cracks in pavements and patios. It has stubborn, mat-like roots that can be hard to pull out in one go – or at all. Leaves are trifoliate, like a shamrock, and are green or burgundy – the latter is the purple variant, which by my (unscientific) observations appears to be the dominant variety in south-east England. The small flowers are a bright egg-yolk yellow.

Perks • The purple variety, particularly, has its charms – that rich colour, and its similarity to the houseplant purple shamrock (*Oxalis triangularis*).

Pitfalls • Despite its tiny size, purple wood sorrel is a feisty little plant with similar explosive seed capsules to bittercress (p. 179). These can be thrust as much as two metres away from the original plant. Although its pint-sized nature means it won't crowd larger plants, you may find yourself pulling it out of paths, gravel drives and beds on a near-daily basis.

Did you know? • This tender weed is sometimes called 'greenhouse weed' because it is so common in glasshouses, surviving frosts in their cosseted warmth.

Curled dock (*Rumex crispus*)

✳	**Flowers**	June to July
✳	**Foliage**	Deciduous
✳	**Height**	1m
✳	**Spread**	20cm
✳	**Preferred conditions**	Sun, dappled shade, partial shade
✳	**Origin**	Europe, Asia, northern Africa
✳	**Toxicity**	Toxic to horses
✳	**Also known as**	Curly dock, yellow dock

Author

How to spot • The leaves of curled dock are easily overlooked – long, oval, often with crinkly edges, they reach a height of only about 30 centimetres. The plant is much easier to spot when the flowers have formed, reaching a height of up to a metre. The flowers themselves are inconspicuous, but held in crowded clusters on branch-like stems that protrude from the main stalk. Even easier to spot are the brown seed heads that follow the flowers. A close relative, broad-leaved dock (*Rumex obtusifolius*), is also widespread.

Perks • If there are stinging nettles (p. 205) nearby, dock can be a handy companion to have on hand – crush a leaf and rub against nettle rash to soothe the sting.

Pitfalls • Both curled dock and its cousin broad-leaved dock are included in the 1959 Weeds Act because they can turn invasive quickly.

Did you know? • Keen foragers recommend adding dock leaves to soups.

Dandelion (*Taraxacum officinale*)

Author

✳	**Flowers**	March to November
✳	**Foliage**	Evergreen
✳	**Height**	45cm
✳	**Spread**	50cm
✳	**Preferred conditions**	Sun, dappled shade, partial shade
✳	**Origin**	Northern Hemisphere
✳	**Toxicity**	No reported toxicity
✳	**Also known as**	Blowball, cankerweed, cankerwort, fairy clock, heart-fever grass, horse gowan, Irish daisy, lion's teeth, milk gowan, pee in the bed, priest's crown, swine's snout, yellow gowan

How to spot • Dandelion leaves grow in a rosette style, close to the ground. They're normally green in colour but can take on a reddish tint in the winter months. In spring, the rosette sends up short stems, topped with fat buds that quickly open to yellow, many-petalled flowers. Once the plant is ready to set seed, the familiar dandelion clocks – a mass of hairy, greyish-white fluff – form.

Perks • While weed-adverse gardeners of the past might have advised pouring boiling water – or something much more toxic – onto dandelion heads, today we know they're a vital source of pollen for bees and other insects. The yellow flowers are a cheerful addition to a patch of grass, with the clock-like seed heads providing a dose of childhood nostalgia.

Pitfalls • If you're not so keen, use a dandelion fork to remove the plants. The leaves grow too close to the ground to mow them off. Removing flowers before they go to seed will also prevent their spread.

Did you know? • As well as being edible raw, the plant's flowers and roots can be used to flavour home-brewed dandelion wine or tea.

Deadnettle (*Lamium purpureum* and *Lamium album*)

Lamium album. *Author*

* Flowers	March to October
* Foliage	Deciduous
* Height	50cm
* Spread	30cm
* Preferred conditions	Partial shade
* Origin	Europe, Asia
* Toxicity	No reported toxicity
* Also known as	Blind nettle, hedge nettle, white or purple archangel

How to spot • Deadnettle tends to pop up anywhere the earth has been disturbed, so you're likely to find it on waste ground, allotments and in cultivated borders. It looks quite like a stinging nettle (p. 205), but as the name suggests, it thankfully has no sting. Red deadnettle (*Lamium purpureum*) has furry, heart-shaped leaves and hooded, reddish-purple flowers that bloom continuously from spring until autumn. White deadnettle (*Lamium album*) exhibits creamy white flowers from March to December. These have a complex, lipped construction and appear on either side of the stem above the leaves.

Lamium purpureum. *Author*

Perks • Red deadnettle is a useful food source for many long-tongued pollinators, including bumblebees and the red mason bee. Meanwhile, the appearance of white deadnettle is so sought after in flowers that many cultivated varieties of *Lamium* have been bred and are sold widely in garden centres.

Did you know? • Deadnettles originated on the European mainland and in Asia, but historians have found traces of the plant in deposits of barley from the Bronze Age in England, suggesting it was brought to the British Isles around that time.

Dog rose (*Rosa canina*)

Daniel Pintilei

✴	**Flowers**	June to July
✴	**Foliage**	Deciduous
✴	**Height**	4m
✴	**Spread**	2.5m
✴	**Preferred conditions**	Sun
✴	**Origin**	Europe, North Africa, Asia
✴	**Toxicity**	No reported toxicity
✴	**Also known as**	Bird briar, briar rose, buckieberries, canker, canker flower, canker rose, cankerberry, cat whin, choop tree, common brier, dog briar, hep briar, hep rose, hep tree, wild rose

Rose hips. *Author*

How to spot • Dog rose is the UK's most abundant wild rose. It is most often found on the edge of woodlands, in hedgerows and deserted scrubland, but also in gardens and allotments. It has spiny, arching stems that can grow to heights of up to four metres and cupped, pale pink or white flowers that appear in May and June. Flowers have five petals and a pleasant, but not overpowering, scent. In the autumn, fat ruby-red rose hips appear. Dog roses are often seen rambling up trees or shrubs for support, using their curved thorns to grip onto branches.

Perks • The flowers are a rich source of nectar for insect life – and a beautiful sight to behold. Glossy rose hips provide interest in autumn and a source of food for birds, and can even be turned into a natural cough syrup rich in vitamin C for us humans.

Pitfalls • Dog roses can stifle the growth of shrubs they scramble up. Due to their potential height, dog roses may need pruning to be kept to size – and those large thorns mean thick gloves are recommended.

Did you know? • The name harks back to a time when it was believed that administering the root to a person bitten by a rabid dog could save their life.

Dog violet (*Viola riviniana*)

Michael Figiel

✳ **Flowers**	April to June	
✳ **Foliage**	Evergreen	
✳ **Height**	10cm	
✳ **Spread**	50cm	
✳ **Preferred conditions**	Sun, partial shade, shade	
✳ **Origin**	Europe, Africa	
✳ **Toxicity**	No reported toxicity	
✳ **Also known as**	Common dog violet, wood violet	

How to spot • If you see a petite purple flower that you think is a violet growing in English woodland, it's likely to be a dog violet. They also are prone to pop up in wilder gardens and lawns in rural areas. The heart-shaped leaves give way to a handsome, true purple flower with a striped white and mauve centre. Unlike the sweet violet (*Viola odorata*), the dog violet has no perfume.

Perks • Dog violets are unfussy flowers: they thrive as well in sun as in shade, and are easy for even the most laidback gardeners to maintain. They make a pretty addition to cottage gardens, shady lawns and the front of borders, and deadheading can prolong their flowering period.

Pitfalls • Slugs and snails love them just as much as many people do, and will munch on buds, flowers and foliage whenever they come across them. Some also find their appearance a little straggly compared to the more rounded sweet violets, and the lack of scent a disappointment.

Did you know? • The Ancient Greeks saw dog violets as a symbol of romance, an association that's spanned the test of time: they also represent 'delicacy in love' in Victorian floriography (the language of flowers).

Enchanter's nightshade (*Circaea lutetiana*)

✳	**Flowers**	June to September
✳	**Foliage**	Deciduous
✳	**Height**	60cm
✳	**Spread**	50cm
✳	**Preferred conditions**	Dappled shade
✳	**Origin**	Europe
✳	**Toxicity**	No reported toxicity
✳	**Also known as**	Enchantress's nightshade, mandrake

Bryony Bowie

How to spot • This woodland plant is most often found in garden beds in the shade or in wooded areas. It has soft, dark green leaves, which appear on opposite sides of its stems. The pinkish-white blooms flower between June and September, and rarely measure more than 5mm in diameter. The seed heads that follow are green and hooked, like burrs.

Perks • If this plant does pop up in the garden, it's very easily tugged out by hand, and it rarely becomes a pervasive problem. The diminutive flowers are quite pretty, so you may prefer to leave it be. It's also sought after by pollinators, especially halictid bees.

Pitfalls • It spreads quickly through its overwintering rhizomes, so can become a problem in gardens if left unchecked. It's also undeniably much more foliage than flower!

Did you know? • Despite its name, enchanter's nightshade is not related to the poisonous plant deadly nightshade (*Atropa belladonna*). It's actually a member of the willowherb family and is not fatally poisonous, although it should not be ingested.

Fat hen (*Chenopodium album*)

Author

★ **Flowers**	June to October	
★ **Foliage**	Deciduous	
★ **Height**	1m	
★ **Spread**	50cm	
★ **Preferred conditions**	Sun, dappled shade, partial shade	
★ **Origin**	Europe, Asia	
★ **Toxicity**	Toxic to horses	
★ **Also known as**	Bacon weed, blackweed, common goosefoot, dirtweed, dirty Dick, frost blite, lamb's quarters, midden meals, muck weed, mutton tops, pigweed, white goosefoot, white spinach	

Author

How to spot • There are several varieties of speedwell found in lawns, flower beds, between paving stones and in gravel. The majority are united by their low-growing, creeping habit, trailing stems, and blueish-purple flowers. Slender speedwell (*Veronica filiformis*) has bright blue flowers that appear between March and May in lawns, while germander speedwell (*Veronica chamaedrys*) forms dense mats of foliage between March and late summer.

Perks • if you're a bit more relaxed about the state of your turf, the plants do offer benefits to insects. Solitary bees are partial to germander speedwell. And the blue flowers add a lovely, bright blue touch in spring.

Pitfalls • For allotment holders and lawn lovers, speedwell can become a troublesome weed: it spreads quickly and can get out of hand as it grows low enough to avoid the blades of a mower. Improving the quality of your grass is one method of control. On allotments, where soil is earmarked for fruit and vegetables, it's probably best to remove speedwell before it takes over.

Did you know? • In the past, spotting germander speedwell on a journey was seen as a symbol of good luck for the traveller. This may well be the source of the name 'speedwell'.

Giant hogweed (*Heracleum mantegazzianum*)

Terry Robinson

✶ **Flowers**	June to August
✶ **Foliage**	Deciduous
✶ **Height**	5m
✶ **Spread**	2m
✶ **Preferred conditions**	Sun
✶ **Origin**	Asia
✶ **Toxicity**	Toxic to humans, cats, dogs and horses
✶ **Also known as**	Cow parsnip, giant cow parsley

How to spot • Giant hogweed looks like a soaring version of cow parsley (*Anthriscus sylvestris*, p. 158). In fact, it's often called giant cow parsley or cow parsnip in tribute. In contrast to that familiar umbellifer, giant hogweed grows up to five metres tall, sporting enormous clusters of cream flowers. Serrated foliage is also huge and often has a purple tint. Leaves can measure an enormous 1.5-3 metres.

Pitfalls • Although the umbel-like, pale flowers of giant hogweed are in line with current floral trends (think wild carrot, p. 213, but supersized) and it was popular in Victorian gardens, the plant falls under Schedule 9 of the Wildlife and Countryside Act 1981 in England, Scotland and Wales. This means it is an offence to plant or encourage its spread in the wild. And this is for very good reason: contact with the leaves has a curious, and devastating, effect on human skin. The sap causes extreme sensitivity to light, which can result in large, painful burns.

Did you know? • There is a smaller type – known simply as hogweed (*Heracleum sphondylium*), which is less toxic and smaller, yet has the same pretty cloud-like flowers.

Great mullein (*Verbascum thapsus*)

✳	**Flowers**	June to August
✳	**Foliage**	Deciduous
✳	**Height**	2m
✳	**Spread**	50cm
✳	**Preferred conditions**	Sun
✳	**Origin**	Europe, Asia
✳	**Toxicity**	No reported toxicity
✳	**Also known as**	Aaron's rod, Adam's flannel, leaf, beggar's blanket, blanket leaf, bullock's lungwort, candlewick, clown's lungwort, common mullein, cow's lungwort, duffle, felt, flannel leaf, flannel plant, hag taper, hag's taper, hare's beard, hedge taper, high taper, Jacob's staff, Jupiter's staff, king's taper, lady's candles, lady's foxglove, lamb's wool, light of the Lord, lucernaria, mullein dock, old man's flannel, rag paper, shepherd's club, torch lily, torches, velvet dock, velvet leaf, velvet plant, white mullein, woollens, woundweed

How to spot • Reaching a height of two metres great mullein is a biennial plant that is difficult to miss. It's most commonly found on waste ground, meadow edges and in gardens. The long, oval leaves are a furry greyish-green – they should feel velvety – and form in whorls close to the bottom of the flowering stem. Yellow flower clusters decorate the top of the plant's tall stalks in its second year. These then turn to green seed pods.

Perks • Great mullein is a grand statement plant that draws the eye, as well as a wealth of wildlife such as the mullein moth and carder bees (the latter using the plant's woolly foliage to build their nests).

Pitfalls • As it grows into a large plant, consider uprooting and moving to somewhere it can stretch its metaphorical legs if it's popped up somewhere it will be constrained.

The plant self-seeds freely, like foxgloves (p. 74), but once you learn to spot its seedlings, you can remove them if preferred.

Did you know? • The plant's many vernacular names often reference light because the Romans used to dip the flower spires in animal fat for use as candles.

Author

Green alkanet (*Pentaglottis sempervirens*)

Author

✳ **Flowers**	March to July
✳ **Foliage**	Evergreen
✳ **Height**	1m
✳ **Spread**	1m
✳ **Preferred conditions**	Partial shade, shade
✳ **Origin**	Europe
✳ **Toxicity**	No reported toxicity
✳ **Also known as**	Evergreen alkanet, evergreen bugloss

How to spot • Perhaps the defining characteristic of this garden interloper – aside from its tenacity – is its hairiness. Reach out to touch it and you'll notice fuzzy stems, leaves and flower buds. The tiny, bright blue flowers have a white centre, and the leaves often sport signs of rust, manifesting in reddish-brown streaks and blotches. You're likely to find it on clay soil and in areas where the soil has not been enriched or cared for.

Perks • Green alkanet will grow in places that fussier plants would turn their noses up at, so you may find it useful in some areas if it can be contained.

Pitfalls • But that's easier said than done. While the flowers are pleasing enough and a hit with pollinators, green alkanet can become very inconvenient due to its tendency to spread. It can regenerate from even the smallest piece of root.

Did you know? • Green alkanet is a member of the same family as borage, hence the similar blue flowers.

Ground elder (*Aegopodium podagraria*)

✳ **Flowers**	May to August
✳ **Foliage**	Deciduous
✳ **Height**	1m
✳ **Spread**	1.5m
✳ **Preferred conditions**	Partial shade, shade
✳ **Origin**	Europe, North America
✳ **Toxicity**	No reported toxicity
✳ **Also known as**	Bishop's weed, goutweed, ground ash, masterwort

Author

How to spot • The shoots have dark green leaves and start to rise above the soil in early spring. The leaves, which are generally seen in groups of five or seven, resemble those of the elder tree (*Sambucus nigra*, p. 110). Although they bear no relation to one another, the likeness inspired ground elder's name. In late spring and throughout summer, umbels of white flowers appear. These mimic the appearance of cow parsley (p. 158) and similar umbellifers. Digging around the plant, you will find a tangle of thin, white roots stretching deep into the soil. These break easily, making them near impossible to remove in one piece.

Perks • Lace-like flowers in creamy white? If it weren't for ground elder's less positive traits, the blooms wouldn't look amiss in a cottage garden.

John Johnston

Pitfalls • Ground elder is a dogged plant and is generally impossible to remove in one go. While most 'weeds' can be lived alongside, even enjoyed, ground elder can regrow from tiny fragments of root and spreads by sending out underground shoots. This means it can spread quickly under fences or sneak in via compost or potted plants. While ground elder may not pose a problem on disused land and the flowers are far from unpleasant, it will take over swiftly wherever it is found – occupying areas earmarked for growing vegetables, flowers, or other uses, so it is more difficult to live alongside compared to other unwanted garden plants.

Did you know? • Ground elder was thought to have medicinal benefits and used to treat gout in the medieval period.

Groundsel (*Senecio vulgaris*)

Author

✳	**Flowers**	January to December
✳	**Foliage**	Deciduous
✳	**Height**	40cm
✳	**Spread**	50cm
✳	**Preferred conditions**	Sun
✳	**Origin**	Europe
✳	**Toxicity**	Toxic to humans, cats, dogs and horses
✳	**Also known as**	Birdseed, chickenweed, chickweed, flower of St Macarius, grinsel, old-man-in-the-spring, ragweed, simson

How to spot • Groundsel has a soft spot for damp, heavy earth, so you'll find it most often in areas of clay soil. It is a very common sight in gardens, allotments and anywhere the ground has been dug over. It is small in stature and its green leaves have a glossy shine with spiky ragged curves. The small macaroni-shaped green and yellow flowers quickly turn to fluffy seed heads. You'll see it flowering throughout the year.

Perks • Pollinators including wasps, bees and butterflies enjoy groundsel's sunny flower heads, and those tubular flowers have an intriguing, unusual appearance.

Pitfalls • The plant can set seed five to six times a year, so it can spread its seedlings across bare soil quite quickly, but is easily removed by hand. It is also a danger to pets and poisonous to humans if ingested.

Did you know? • Groundsel is closely related to ragwort (p. 197).

Hairy bittercress (*Cardamine hirsuta*)

Author

✳	**Flowers**	March to December
✳	**Foliage**	Deciduous
✳	**Height**	30cm
✳	**Spread**	30cm
✳	**Preferred conditions**	Sun
✳	**Origin**	Europe
✳	**Toxicity**	No reported toxicity
✳	**Also known as**	Lamb's cress, land cress, touch-me-not

How to spot • This is a very widespread plant throughout the UK – you'll find it in beds, borders, paths, lawns, at the edges of walls and popping up in plant pots. It is a small plant, growing to just a few centimetres in height, although the stems that hold the flowers can occasionally reach 30 centimetres long. It has a rosette of rounded, hairy leaves and petite white flowers on skinny, branching stalks.

Perks • Hairy bittercress is a member of the mustard (*Brassicaceae*) family and, like its relatives broccoli and cabbage, is edible. Foragers suggest trying it in salads: it has a bitter tang, a bit like endive or watercress.

Pitfalls • Although this is a pint-sized plant, its ability to flower almost all year gives it a distinct advantage in the spreading stakes. Its explosive seed pods mean its seeds can spread up to one metre away from the parent plant, or much further if carried on the wind. Remove seedlings before they flower to prevent spreading. Small specimens are easily forked out.

Did you know? • Rub a leaf of this plant between your fingers and you'll understand why it carries the adjective 'hairy' – minuscule hairs cover the foliage.

Hart's tongue fern (*Asplenium scolopendrium*)

✳	**Foliage**	Evergreen
✳	**Height**	50cm
✳	**Spread**	50cm
✳	**Preferred conditions**	Shade
✳	**Origin**	Northern Hemisphere
✳	**Toxicity**	No reported toxicity
✳	**Also known as**	Burnt weed, buttonhole, Christ's hair

Sally Jennings

How to spot • Hart's tongue fern is a widespread fern of damp and shady woodland, where it will often grow en masse under the tree canopy. It is also common to see it growing out of old walls, and in shady gardens. This evergreen fern has crinkly, glossy green leaves, roughly similar in shape to a palette knife. The rusty brown spores are visible underneath the leaves.

Perks • Happy in shade and also happy enough to do its thing without much human input (as its presence in woodland and walls confirms), hart's tongue fern is an elegant and slow-growing addition to a shady border.

Pitfalls • If it's been mistakenly planted in full sun, the foliage will crisp up and the plant will suffer – but it's simple to dig up and move with a sharp spade.

Did you know? • Ferns reproduce by spores on the underside of the leaves. When the spores reach maturity, they are ejected and carried by the wind.

Herb Robert (*Geranium robertianum*)

Author

✳	**Flowers**	May to September
✳	**Foliage**	Deciduous
✳	**Height**	50cm
✳	**Spread**	50cm
✳	**Preferred conditions**	Dappled shade, partial shade, shade
✳	**Origin**	Europe
✳	**Toxicity**	No reported toxicity
✳	**Also known as**	Crow's foot, death-comes-quickly, dragon's blood, fox geranium, fox grass, Jenny Wren, kiss-me-quick, knife and fork, little bachelor's buttons, little red robin, nightingales, pink bird's eye, pink pinafore, red bird's eye, red robin, redshanks, Robert's geranium, St Robert's herb, stinking Bob, wren flower

How to spot • Look for herb Robert in shady spaces, where it is often found sprawling across the soil. It is a low-growing, airy plant with deeply divided green foliage that often becomes tinged with – or occasionally, entirely – dark red as the plant ages. Delicate pale pink flowers appear between May and September. When rubbed between one's fingers, the leaves emit a pungent odour not dissimilar to rubber tyres – hence its American nickname, 'stinking Bob'.

Perks • I have a real soft spot for this self-seeder, which flowers as prettily as many cultivated geraniums and has attractively coloured foliage.

Pitfalls • Some gardeners report an itchy rash when handling, so if you do decide to pull it up, remember to wear gloves and long sleeves. If you decide to leave it be, it's easy to weed out should you change your mind later – although it may make itself at home by spreading out in the meantime.

Did you know? • The 'Robert' in herb Robert is said to refer to Saint Robert, an eleventh-century French monk and herbalist.

Horsetail (*Equisetum arvense*)

Author

✳ **Foliage**		Semi-evergreen
✳ **Height**		1.5m
✳ **Spread**		70cm
✳ **Preferred conditions**		Sun, dappled shade, partial shade
✳ **Origin**		Northern Hemisphere
✳ **Toxicity**		Toxic to humans and horses
✳ **Also known as**		Bottlebrush, mare's tail, scouring rush

Andreas Brunn

How to spot • The first time I saw horsetail in the wild, alongside the Thames Path in great, swaying thickets, I thought it had a mystic, primitive beauty and immediately tried to find out its name when I got home. And that unworldly appearance might be because these plants hark back to another age – *Equisetum* dates back to the Early Jurassic period. This deep-rooted plant looks like the beginnings of a fir tree, with bristly green stems.

Pitfalls • Horsetail is known to spread so rapidly that it is unwise to risk a full-scale takeover. As it spreads by rhizomes, new plants can spring up several metres away from the original, in between pavers or in lawns as well as open soil, so it's worth staying on top of their spread if you'd like to grow other things, too. Once established, keeping horsetail from taking over is much more difficult.

Did you know? • If you rub a piece of horsetail between your fingers, you'll notice a gritty feel – that's because the plants contain grains of silica, the main component in sand.

Ivy (*Hedera* spp.)

*	**Flowers**	September to November
*	**Foliage**	Evergreen
*	**Height**	12m
*	**Spread**	4m
*	**Preferred conditions**	Partial shade, shade
*	**Origin**	Europe
*	**Toxicity**	Toxic to humans, cats, dogs and horses
*	**Also known as**	Bentwood, bindwood

How to spot • Ivy is a recognisable plant thanks to its ubiquity, frequently seen trailing over fences, climbing up tree trunks or sprawling across open ground. The dark green, glossy leaves differ in shape depending on variety. Cream clusters of flowers, often visited by bees, appear from September to November. Common ivy (*Hedera helix*) has three- or five-lobed leaves, often variegated, and black berries in the winter.

Perks • Ivy will grow almost anywhere and keeps its leaves all year which makes it a useful plant for winter interest. Equally, it offers many benefits to British wildlife: birds enjoy the berries, bees love the autumn flowers and bats use the shrub as a nesting site.

Pitfalls • Its ability to colonise bare soil with its persistent aerial roots that form along the stems can become a real problem if left to grow unchecked over years. It will take nutrients and water away from other plants and make it difficult to plant other things as the soil is clogged with roots. Keeping it in check with regular pruning is a good way to avoid this.

Author

Did you know? • Ivy has also been shown to help us humans: by growing it up a wall, it can help to regulate the temperature of buildings in summer and reduce moisture in winter.

Ivy-leaved toadflax (*Cymbalaria muralis*)

✳ **Flowers**	April to October
✳ **Foliage**	Semi-evergreen
✳ **Height**	10cm
✳ **Spread**	50cm
✳ **Preferred conditions**	Sun, dappled shade
✳ **Origin**	the Mediterranean
✳ **Toxicity**	No reported toxicity
✳ **Also known as**	Climbing sailor, Coliseum ivy, devil's ribbon, ivy weed, ivy wort, Kenilworth ivy, Kentucky ivy, Oxford ivy, Oxford weed, penny leaf, roving sailor, wandering sailor, travelling sailor

Author

How to spot • Blink and you'll miss it – this small perennial herb is incredibly petite, reaching a height of just ten centimetres. It is usually found growing in cracks, crevices and small holes in brick walls, making it even more likely to go unnoticed. But once you know where to look it's usually easy to identify by its slightly shiny, lobed leaves (a similar shape to ivy, p. 185) and mauve flowers that resemble tiny snapdragons (p. 90).

Perks • I have a soft spot for the tenacity of this diminutive plant, growing as it does in dry, inhospitable places. It can add interest and understated beauty wherever it pops up. It's also pollinated by bees, who enjoy its flowers.

Pitfalls • If you'd rather pristine brickwork or pavers, its rapid spreading may be a nuisance, but it's easy enough to pull out and compost.

Did you know? • The plant hitched a lift to the UK from the Mediterranean in the 1600s, probably on a boat – hence its nickname 'Travelling Sailor'. It's also sometimes known as 'Oxford Weed' because it is thought to have made its inaugural journey to Britain on board a shipment of statues that were sent from Italy to Oxford, and quickly became established in the walled gardens of the city of dreaming spires.

Japanese knotweed (*Reynoutria japonica*)

Melissa McMasters

✶ **Flowers**	July to September
✶ **Foliage**	Deciduous
✶ **Height**	3m
✶ **Spread**	7m
✶ **Preferred conditions**	Sun, dappled shade
✶ **Origin**	Asia
✶ **Toxicity**	No reported toxicity
✶ **Also known as**	Donkey rhubarb, Hancock's curse, pea-shooter plant

How to spot • The hollow stems of Japanese knotweed look a little like bamboo (p. 98) and grow incredibly quickly – up to 20 centimetres a day in spring and summer. Young leaves are red, but soon turn to green. These are displayed in a zigzag-like alternating pattern up the stems. The cream flower clusters begin to appear towards the end of July. By mid-autumn, the plant will die back to ground level, before returning with renewed vigour the following year.

Pitfalls • Japanese knotweed is so doggedly persistent that – in the UK, at least – homeowners and landlords have a legal obligation to prevent its spread to neighbouring land. It is so tenacious that it can break through concrete and drains. If you find Japanese knotweed on land you're responsible for it's best to call in the professionals, as the roots can reach up to three metres deep.

Did you know? • There are four types of invasive knotweed in the UK described by the government, but Japanese knotweed is the most well-known.

Lesser celandine (*Ficaria verna*)

✷	**Flowers**	January to April
✷	**Foliage**	Deciduous
✷	**Height**	50cm
✷	**Spread**	50cm
✷	**Preferred conditions**	Partial shade, shade
✷	**Origin**	Europe, Asia, northern Africa
✷	**Toxicity**	Toxic to humans, cats, dogs and horses
✷	**Also known as**	Fig buttercup, pilewort

How to spot • Lesser celandine is a common spring flower, seen carpeting damp spots such as riverbanks and woodland, as well as in gardens and hedgerows. The plant sports glossy, heart-shaped foliage and small, teacup-shaped yellow flowers that often blanket wide areas. Each flower has between eight and twelve shiny petals, and will fade to a creamy white as the season progresses.

Perks • The flower has a lot of value to wildlife, as one of the earliest to make an appearance in spring, and provides pollen and nectar for bumblebees and small beetles. While the plant can spread quite quickly, it's well suited to wooded and wilder gardens, and provides useful ground cover quickly. Plus its short growing season – even the leaves die back around April – means it simply doesn't have the time to cause too much havoc!

Bryony Bowie

Pitfalls • Lesser celandine is poisonous to humans if ingested. The tuberous roots allow it to spread quickly, especially in disturbed earth.

Did you know? • The writer William Wordsworth (1770–1850) was clearly a fan. He wrote three poems about the plant: *The Small Celandine*, *To the Same Flower* and *To the Small Celandine*.

Mallow (*Malva sylvestris*)

✳	**Flowers**	June to October
✳	**Foliage**	Semi-evergreen
✳	**Height**	1.5m
✳	**Spread**	1m
✳	**Preferred conditions**	Sun
✳	**Origin**	Europe
✳	**Toxicity**	No reported toxicity
✳	**Also known as**	Cheese cakes, cheese flower, cheeses, high mallow, hock, hock herb, marsh mallow, mauls, maws, round dock

How to spot • Commonly spotted on roadsides and neglected land, this perennial weed has hairy stems and subtly striped, mauve-coloured blooms with five petals per flower. Leaves are rounded in shape, like hollyhocks (*Alcea rosea*, p. 77). It is found throughout

Author

the British Isles but is particularly abundant in Wales and the south of England.

Perks • Mallow flowers resemble several other flowers that gardeners choose to plant and nurture in their gardens (like hollyhock, and rose of Sharon, p. 140), plus they're a hit with pollinators. Their long flowering period makes them valuable additions to a wilder garden. And the leaves can even be brewed into a gardener's tea.

Pitfalls • Mallow has an extremely deep tap root that is difficult to remove, so if you want to get rid of it, prepare for it to take several tries – or extreme strength.

Did you know? • The word for the colour 'mauve' derives from the mallow plant – from the Latin 'malva'.

Ox-eye daisy (*Leucanthemum vulgare*)

✳	**Flowers**	June to September
✳	**Foliage**	Deciduous
✳	**Height**	1m
✳	**Spread**	50cm
✳	**Preferred conditions**	Sun
✳	**Origin**	Europe, Asia
✳	**Toxicity**	Toxic to cats and dogs
✳	**Also known as**	Big daisy, bull daisy, dog daisy, dun daisy, espibawn, field daisy, herb Margaret, horse daisy, horse gowan, large white gowan, love-me, love-me-not, marguerite, mathes, maudlinwort, midsummer daisy, moon daisy, moon flower, moon penny, poor-land daisy, pretty maids, sheriff pink, white cap, white daisy, white goldes, white ox-eye, white weed

Author

How to spot • Think of the common fried egg-like daisies found in lawns, then super-size them. Although they're not massive by any standards, with the flowers reaching around five centimetres in width. They tend to thrive on roadside verges and in meadows and are easy to identify thanks to their white petals circling a domed yellow centre. They're also found in borders.

Perks • The ox-eye daisy's yellow flower heads hold valuable nectar for pollinators, and if you don't mind them spreading a little, the flowers make for a cheerful sight and have a long flowering period.

Pitfalls • In its favoured conditions the ox-eye daisy can take over quickly in a border, at the expense of other perennial plants. It's best to contain it or site it in an area where you don't mind its advances.

Did you know? • Ox-eye daisies are the largest members of the daisy family native to the UK.

Petty spurge (*Euphorbia peplus*)

Author

✳	**Flowers**	April to October
✳	**Foliage**	Deciduous
✳	**Height**	30cm
✳	**Spread**	30cm
✳	**Preferred conditions**	Sun, dappled shade, partial shade
✳	**Origin**	Europe, Asia, North Africa
✳	**Toxicity**	Toxic to humans, cats, dogs and horses
✳	**Also known as**	Cancer weed, milkweed, radium weed

How to spot • Petty spurge is found on ground that has been dug over, so is an expected sight in gardens and on allotments and building sites. It is small, reaching a height of around 30cm, and has lime green leaves born on thin, branching stems. Its flowers are also small and of a lime green colour.

Perks • The cultivated Mediterranean version is frequently seen in garden borders, where it can grow quite large and sometimes take over – if you like the look, why not consider keeping the smaller 'weedy' version, considered a more manageable plant with comparable aesthetics.

Pitfalls • However, beware if your garden is visited by curious pets or children – petty spurge produces a white, milky sap when its stems are broken that can be toxic if it enters the eyes.

Did you know? • The sap is so powerful, however, that it has recently been used to develop treatments for cancerous skin conditions by US pharmaceutical companies.

Poppy (*Papaver rhoeas*)

Author

✳	**Flowers**	June to August
✳	**Foliage**	Deciduous
✳	**Height**	1m
✳	**Spread**	50cm
✳	**Preferred conditions**	Sun
✳	**Origin**	Europe, North Africa, Asia
✳	**Toxicity**	Toxic to dogs No reported toxicity
✳	**Also known as**	Corn poppy, corn rose, field poppy, Flanders poppy, red poppy

How to spot • Look for common poppies where the soil has been disturbed and their seeds exposed to light. They're frequent visitors to allotments and gardens in rural areas where the ground has been recently dug over, and often pop up where wildflower mixes have been scattered. The flowers are an unmissable bright red – familiar to many for their role in Remembrance Day commemorations – and stems are hairy in texture with deeply lobed leaves.

Perks • Field poppies are rarer than they once were due to the rise of intensive agriculture – they used to be a familiar sight on field edges and farmland. If you find them on your patch, count your blessings, and enjoy the way they slot in nicely among ornamental perennials. Bumblebees are very fond of the nectar-rich flowers.

Pitfalls • The poppy is vulnerable to several diseases as well as attack by aphids. And like all poppies, the delicate flowers are short-lived.

Did you know? • Poppies' association with remembrance, and especially the First World War, are well documented. The reason why field poppies thrived in Flanders' fields, however, was because of the extent to which trench warfare disturbed the soil – creating the poppy's ideal growing habitat.

Primrose (*Primula vulgaris*)

Bryony Bowie

✳	**Flowers**	December to May
✳	**Foliage**	Semi-evergreen
✳	**Height**	10cm
✳	**Spread**	10cm
✳	**Preferred conditions**	Sun, dappled shade, partial shade, shade
✳	**Origin**	Europe, Africa, Asia
✳	**Toxicity**	Toxic to cats, dogs and horses
✳	**Also known as**	Common primrose, English primrose, primula

How to spot • The cheery little flower heads of primrose are easy to spot, blooming at a time when many other flowering plants are still sleeping off the winter. The dark green leaves grow in a rosette pattern, with each leaf in the shape of an elongated lozenge. The five-notched flowers are usually pale yellow, with a darker yellow centre, but garden centres now sell cultivated varieties in all sorts of shades.

Perks • Once you have one primula, you will soon have many if the conditions are right – and cross-breeding between plants means they'll pop up in an array of primary school shades. After many years of the classic lemon yellow variety

Marcus Winkler

adorning my plot, I was delighted to see a sherbet pink specimen appear one year. Primroses found in wooded areas are a sign of ancient woodland.

Pitfalls • Primroses can fall victim to a number of bugs, including aphids, slugs and vine weevil. It's common to see foliage and flowers with bites taken out of them. The leaves can also be affected by grey mould.

Did you know? • The name primrose means 'first rose', as the flowers are one of the first spring flowers to appear, and are seen as a promise of warmer days to come.

Purple toadflax (*Linaria purpurea*)

Author

Author

✳	**Flowers**	May to November
✳	**Foliage**	Deciduous
✳	**Height**	1m
✳	**Spread**	50cm
✳	**Preferred conditions**	Sun
✳	**Origin**	the Mediterranean
✳	**Toxicity**	No reported toxicity

How to spot • You're just as likely to spot towers of toadflax on country lanes as you are in gardens, where clumps will readily self-seed. Its narrow, flattened leaves are a muted, almost silver, green. The purple flowers form on upright spires similar to some veronicas and lavender (p. 126), but have a lipped appearance – like snapdragons (p. 90).

Perks • When this wildflower pops up at the back of a bed or near a fence, it makes a graceful addition to a herbaceous border. Cultivated varieties in pink and white are even sold in garden centres nowadays. I fondly call it 'lazy gardener's delphinium'. Beloved by pollinators, it is also the food source of the toadflax brocade moth, rare in the UK.

Pitfalls • If it has self-seeded at the front of a border, its height may cause issues or shade out other plants behind it, but it doesn't particularly mind being dug up and moved. And if you don't like unwanted volunteer plants, you'll be pulling it out again and again if you allow it to flower and set seed even once.

Did you know? • The name toadflax is thought to derive from the resemblance between each flower's open-mouthed appearance and the broad jaw of a toad.

Ragwort (*Senecio jacobaea*)

✳	**Flowers**	July to October
✳	**Foliage**	Deciduous
✳	**Height**	90cm
✳	**Spread**	50cm
✳	**Preferred conditions**	Sun
✳	**Origin**	Europe
✳	**Toxicity**	Toxic to humans, cats, dogs and horses
✳	**Also known as**	Benweed, cankerwort, dog standard, James-wort, mare's fart, ragweed, staggerwort, stammerwort, stinking nanny, stinking willie, tansy ragwort

How to spot • The base of ragwort sports a rosette of large, frilly green leaves. This foliage tends to die back as the bright yellow flowers are coming into bloom. When in flower, identification may also be helped by the presence of the cinnabar caterpillars that like to feed on the plant – these can be up to 3cm long and have distinctive black and orange stripes.

Perks • Ragwort does have at least one loyal champion: the aforementioned cinnabar caterpillar. The plant is its primary food source. It's also popular with bees and other insects.

Pitfalls • Ragwort contains chemicals that are extremely toxic to horses and other livestock. It's no treat for humans either – it can cause skin irritation and burns, so wear gloves and long sleeves when handling. It is not often found in city or suburban

Author

gardens, but it can be very dangerous indeed in paddocks and rural areas where gardens or allotments back onto fields where the affected animals graze.

Did you know? • Ragwort is one of the five harmful weeds on the 1959 Weeds Act and penalties will be levelled against anyone allowing its spread to agricultural land.

Red valerian (*Centranthus ruber*)

✳	**Flowers**	May to October
✳	**Foliage**	Semi-evergreen
✳	**Height**	1m
✳	**Spread**	50cm
✳	**Preferred conditions**	Sun
✳	**Origin**	the Mediterranean
✳	**Toxicity**	No reported toxicity
✳	**Also known as**	Drunkards, fox, fox's brush, German lilac, Jupiter's beard, kiss-me-quick, pretty Betsy, red spur valerian, scarlet lightning, Spanish valerian, spur valerian

How to spot • Find red valerian in garden borders and growing along the edges of pavements, walls and waste ground. It has undivided green leaves that feel plump to the touch, like a succulent. When in bloom, red valerian shows off magenta flower heads made up of many small, five-petalled flowers. Pale pink and white-flowering varieties are also found, although less commonly. By mid- to late summer, the flowers will have gone to seed and left fluffy grey seed heads in their place.

Perks • It offers long-lasting colour in the garden, nourishes bees and butterflies, and is a cardinal joy to spot out in the wild growing in walls and pavement cracks, particularly in Devon and Cornwall. Because the plant is happy growing in very alkaline soil, it doesn't mind the lime in mortar – which is why it's perfect for growing in the cracks of an old wall.

Pitfalls • Red valerian has attracted a reputation for being given an inch and taking a mile, but it's easy enough to pull out if it's growing somewhere unwanted.

Bryony Bowie

Did you know? • This plant shares a name and heritage with common valerian (*Valeriana officinialis*), the herb used in many homoeopathic sedative formulations. But it has none of the same soporific benefits.

Ribwort plantain (*Plantago lanceolata*)

✳	**Flowers**	April to October
✳	**Foliage**	Semi-evergreen
✳	**Height**	50cm
✳	**Spread**	50cm
✳	**Preferred conditions**	Sun
✳	**Origin**	Europe, Asia
✳	**Toxicity**	No reported toxicity
✳	**Also known as**	Black Jack, buckhorn, cat's cradle, chimney-sweeps, cock grass, cocks, dog's ribs, English plantain, headsman, hen plant, jack straws, kemps seed, klops, knock-heads, lamb's tail, leechwort, narrow-leaved plantain, ram's tongue, rat tail, ribgrass, ribwort, ripple grass, windles

Author

How to spot • This is another plant of grasslands, popping up with regularity on the edges of farmland and in meadows as well as garden lawns. The spear-shaped leaves, which can be up to 20cm in length, grow in a rosette formation close to the ground before sending up tiny white flowers on golden-brown flower heads, balanced on sinewy stems.

Perks • I have a soft spot for the flowers, which can be used in dried floral arrangements, and for the seed heads, which provide useful sustenance for goldfinches and other birds over winter. In a wildflower meadow or flower-rich lawn, it makes a pretty addition to a garden.

Pitfalls • Ribwort plantain might be a nuisance if it pops up in a manicured lawn or makes it clear it's enjoying the fertile soil on your allotment, in which case it's easy to pull up by hand (for smaller plants) or using a trowel or fork (for larger specimens).

Did you know? • In the pages of Shakespeare's *Romeo & Juliet*, none other than Romeo himself endorses ribwort plantain as a medicinal herb.

Rosebay willowherb (*Chamaenerion angustifolium*)

✳	**Flowers**	April to October
✳	**Foliage**	Deciduous
✳	**Height**	1.5m
✳	**Spread**	2.5m
✳	**Preferred conditions**	Sun
✳	**Origin**	Northern Hemisphere
✳	**Toxicity**	No reported toxicity
✳	**Also known as**	Bay willow, blooming willow, burntweed, fireweed, French willow, French willowherb, great willowherb, herb wickopy, moose tongue, Persian willow, pigweed, purple rocket, rose bay, rose elder, thunder flower, wickup

How to spot • This tall, eye-catching plant is often found colonising entire hillsides, neglected building sites or areas of woodland. Like many 'weeds', it favours anywhere the earth has been disturbed. It is really quite striking, with the look and architectural aesthetic qualities of a sought-after garden plant. Its green leaves curve around the stalk like a spiral staircase, with large magenta flower spikes at the top of the stem. These are followed by long, slender seed pods.

Perks • Rosebay willowherb's architectural flowers, rising to altitudes of over a metre, are a powerful sight – and their colour, too, is arresting.

Eleanor Burfitt

Pitfalls • Unfortunately, the plant spreads very quickly by rhizomes and can become established – and difficult to remove – at a startling speed. Each plant also produces up to 80,000 seeds. For this reason, it's not recommended for small gardens, allotments or veg patches – although in a large, wild garden, you could consider leaving it to do its thing.

Did you know? • Rosebay willowherb is sometimes known as fireweed, burntweed or bombweed. This is because it was common to see the plant flowering in huge drifts on derelict bomb sites during and directly after the Second World War.

Selfheal (*Prunella vulgaris*)

✳	Flowers	June to October
✳	Foliage	Semi-evergreen
✳	Height	30cm
✳	Spread	50cm
✳	Preferred conditions	Sun, partial shade
✳	Origin	Europe, Asia, America
✳	Toxicity	No reported toxicity
✳	Also known as	Blue curls, blue Lucy, brownwort, brunel, caravaun bog, carpenter grass, carpenter's herb, carpenter's square, heart of the earth, heal-all, herb carpenter, Hercules' all-heal, hook-heal, hookweed, panay, proud carpenter, sickle-heal, sicklewort, slough-heal, square stem, thimble flower

How to spot • You'll often find this diminutive plant crawling along the soil in wooded and grassy areas and in unmown garden lawns. It grows happily across the British Isles. It is small in stature, reaching just 30 centimetres in height, and bears small, cylindrical, deep purple flowers on short, upright stems.

Perks • Unless you're a member of the stripy lawn brigade, a little selfheal in the lawn won't harm anyone and the pop of purple is a welcome sight – plus it will likely nourish more than a few bees and butterflies in the process.

Pitfalls • Selfheal can spread quickly in a lawn, even one that is mowed regularly, outcompeting grass in certain circumstances. Dig out with a fork if it is growing somewhere you'd rather it didn't.

Author

Did you know? • The names carpenter's herb and hook-heal are thought to originate from the fact that the corolla looks like a bill hook in profile, a traditional tool used in forestry. Some have also posited that carpenters planted it outside their workshops for treating occupational cuts and bruises.

Sow thistle (*Sonchus* spp.)

✳	**Flowers**	April to October
✳	**Foliage**	Deciduous
✳	**Height**	2.5m
✳	**Spread**	1m
✳	**Preferred conditions**	Sun
✳	**Origin**	Europe, western Asia
✳	**Toxicity**	Toxic to horses
✳	**Also known as**	Milk-thistle, swine thistle

Bryony Bowie

How to spot • Sow thistles come in many shapes and sizes, with the largest kind reaching over two metres in height. The leaves grow in a dandelion-like rosette at the base of the plant and are covered in tiny spines, so remember to don thick gloves if handling. The bold yellow flowers assume the shape of a daisy, reach about two centimetres in diameter and are borne in clusters on tall stems. The seed heads are fluffy and easy to spot.

Pitfalls • These plants produce many seeds in a short space of time, so can spread quickly. Unlike some other wild plants, sow thistle has few uses to humans and its spiny leaves make it an unpleasant garden guest in the lawn or border. You can fork out the plant or remove flower heads before it goes to seed.

Did you know? • Pigs will happily eat sow thistle's prickly leaves – that's how this weed gets its name. The leaves also emit a milky white sap, thought to aid in the production of milk and therefore fed to lactating sows – hence its other common title, milk-thistle.

Stinging nettle (*Urtica dioica* and *Urtica urens*)

✳	**Flowers**	May to September
✳	**Foliage**	Deciduous
✳	**Height**	2m
✳	**Spread**	1m
✳	**Preferred conditions**	Sun, dappled shade, partial shade
✳	**Origin**	Europe, Asia
✳	**Toxicity**	Toxic to dogs
✳	**Also known as**	Common nettle

How to spot • The British Isles are home to two kinds of nettles: a smaller annual nettle (*Urtica urens*) and a taller perennial type (*Urtica dioica*). The latter is more widespread. Plants have pointed leaves with serrated edges, covered in tiny hairs that act like needles when they come into contact with human skin. White flowers appear between May and September. Nettles are commonly found on ground disturbed by human activity.

Perks • At the back of a garden or plot, perhaps, they can be left in peace and their benefits enjoyed by the red admiral butterfly among others. I keep a small patch contained on my allotment to brew into homemade fertiliser. It can also be used in nettle soup or pesto.

Pitfalls • Despite their benefits to wildlife and culinary uses, nothing

Author

can detract from the incontrovertible fact: stinging nettles remain extremely unpleasant to touch and it's unwise to leave them be in areas where there is foot traffic or where children play.

Did you know? • Nettles are loaded with chlorophyll, the green pigment found in plants. So much so that the British government used the plants – collected by civilians – to make a green dye used for camouflaging military uniforms during the Second World War.

Teasel (*Dipsacus fullonum*)

Author

✳	**Flowers**	July to August
✳	**Foliage**	Deciduous
✳	**Height**	2.5m
✳	**Spread**	1.5m
✳	**Preferred conditions**	Sun
✳	**Origin**	Europe, northern Africa, western Asia
✳	**Toxicity**	No reported toxicity
✳	**Also known as**	Card weed, clothier's brush, fuller's teasel, fuller's thistle, gipsy combs, Venus' bath

How to spot • Teasels are dramatic biennial plants, likely to draw attention wherever they are found thanks to their tall stature and spiny seed heads. In the first year, a rosette of coarse, stiff leaves forms near the base, followed in the second year by prickly stems crowned with purple-green, egg-shaped flower heads surrounded by bracts. These turn light green before browning in the autumn and persist throughout the winter. Its name (*Dipsacus*) means 'thirst', as rain collects in cup-like sections where the leaves meet the stem.

Perks • Teasel seed heads are an important source of food for goldfinches. These small, colourful birds can often be seen pulling seeds from the dried flower heads in the autumn. The plants add structural beauty to borders and the dried heads can also be used in floral arrangements.

Pitfalls • In heavy, damp soils like clay, teasel can outcompete other plants and spread quickly. While this makes it ideal for a meadow, it might not be as welcome in your pristine ornamental border. The spiny heads are also unsuitable for the curious, roaming palms of children!

Did you know? • The plant was spread around the world by wool makers, who brought along teasel on their travels. They used the plant to smooth the finish of woollen fabric once woven. This is why the plant is also known as clothier's brush.

Thistle (*Cirsium* spp.)

✳	**Flowers**	July to October
✳	**Foliage**	Evergreen
✳	**Height**	1.5m
✳	**Spread**	Dependent on variety
✳	**Preferred conditions**	Sun
✳	**Origin**	Europe
✳	**Toxicity**	No reported toxicity
✳	**Also known as**	Bank thistle, bird thistle, blue thistle, boar thistle, bull thistle, bur thistle, button thistle, horse thistle, prickly thistle, swamp thistle, way thistle

How to spot • Thistles come in all shapes and sizes, but one thing unites them all: prickles! The leaves, stalks, flowers, and seed heads are all covered in sharp spikes. Most thistles sport a rosette of thorny leaves at the base of the plant, with

Author

tall flowering stems crowned by fluffy purple flowers. Seed heads that follow are usually white and cotton wool-like in appearance.

Perks • Thistles, despite being a barbed hazard to humans, are enjoyed by butterflies. Small birds, goldfinches and siskins especially, are also fond of them.

Pitfalls • Although thistles are dramatic and aesthetically pleasing plants, their spikiness means most would rather not invite them into areas where humans and domestic animals spend time. Creeping thistle (*Cirsium arvense*) and spear thistle (*Cirsium vulgare*) can both spread quickly, and fall under the 1959 Weeds Act. Copious digging – while wearing thick gloves and long sleeves – is needed to remove the plant's deep taproot, which should then be burned or thrown away rather than composted.

Did you know? • This prickly plant is the national emblem of Scotland.

Thrift (*Armeria maritima*)

✳	**Flowers**	June to July
✳	**Foliage**	Evergreen
✳	**Height**	50cm
✳	**Spread**	50cm
✳	**Preferred conditions**	Sun
✳	**Origin**	Europe, North America
✳	**Toxicity**	No reported toxicity
✳	**Also known as**	Cliff rose, cushion pin, gilliflower, lady's cushion, lady's pincushion, marsh daisy, sea cushion, sea grass, sea pink, sea lavender

How to spot • Look for thrift in coastal areas – the clue is in 'maritima', and its common names sea thrift, sea lavender and the like. The plant forms small clumps measuring half a metre tall and wide topped with magenta or lilac flowers, although white cultivars are also sold in garden centres. From afar the plant looks much like a bunch of chives in flower.

Perks • Thanks to its natural cliff and seaside habitat, thrift is a tough plant – as perfectly happy in salt-laced winds as in hot and humid regions. It likes well-drained soil, so is an ideal plant for a rockery, gravel garden or container.

Pitfalls • For all its bubblegum beauty, sea thrift is unsuitable for heavy clay soils and will only do well in full sun. It also has a short – but spellbinding – flowering period.

Tim Green

Did you know? • The British threepence coin depicted a clump of sea thrift from 1937 until the 1950s.

Bryony Bowie

Welsh poppy (*Papaver cambricum* or *Meconopsis cambrica*)

Dannie Jing

*	**Flowers**	June to August
*	**Foliage**	Deciduous
*	**Height**	50cm
*	**Spread**	50cm
*	**Preferred conditions**	Partial shade
*	**Origin**	Europe
*	**Toxicity**	No reported toxicity
*	**Also known as**	Yellow poppy

How to spot • This cheerful poppy is most often found in damp, shady spaces, high up on hills or mountains. You're most likely to spot it – as the name suggests – in Wales and neighbouring south-west England. However, it is also now sold as an herbaceous perennial in garden centres and pops up regularly in gardens around the country. The sunny yellow flowers sport four overlapping petals on long, thin, green stems. The leaves are what's called 'pinnately divided', which means the leaflets are arranged on either side of the stem in pairs opposite each other and look like other plants in the poppy family.

Perks • It's a favourite of hoverflies and bees. Many other poppies (p. 193) are annuals, flowering for just one year, but Welsh poppies have the benefit of returning season after season.

Pitfalls • The flowers don't last long, so enjoy them while you can.

Did you know? • The Welsh poppy is the emblem of the Welsh political party Plaid Cymru.

White bryony (*Bryonia dioica*)

✴	**Flowers**	May to August
✴	**Foliage**	Deciduous
✴	**Height**	4m
✴	**Spread**	3m
✴	**Preferred conditions**	Sun, partial shade
✴	**Origin**	Europe
✴	**Toxicity**	Toxic to humans, cats, dogs and horses
✴	**Also known as**	Devil's cherry, devil's turnip, English mandrake, grapewort, Isle of Wight vine, murrain berries, red bryony, tetterberry, white wild vine, wild hop

How to spot • There's something enchanting, almost fairytale-like, about white bryony's climbing curls of foliage and starry flowers. The hand-shaped leaves have five points, and the flowers are a pretty and delicate creamy white and are followed by burnished red berries in autumn. This is a climbing plant that needs a fence or another plant to scramble up – identification may be helped by looking out for its strong tendrils, with each resembling a tiny, coiled spring.

Perks • As a sprawling, fast-growing climber, white bryony can quickly cover an unsightly wall and fence with its aesthetically pleasing flowers and charmingly shaped leaves.

Author

Pitfalls • In a wild area of the garden, bryony is a beautiful climber, but keep away from areas frequented by curious little ones or animals – this plant is highly poisonous. In cultivated areas, bryony will also quickly smother other plants.

Did you know? • White bryony is a member of the *Cucurbitaceae* family of plants – making it Britain's only native member of the cucumber family.

White clover (*Trifolium repens*)

Author

✶	**Flowers**	May to October
✶	**Foliage**	Semi-evergreen
✶	**Height**	50cm
✶	**Spread**	50cm
✶	**Preferred conditions**	Sun
✶	**Origin**	Europe, Asia
✶	**Toxicity**	Toxic to horses
✶	**Also known as**	Clover grass, common clover, creeping clover, Dutch clover, gowan, honey stalks, honeysuckle grass, lamb's suckling, shamrock

How to spot • White clover is very common in grassy areas – from playing fields to garden lawns – and forms large mats of foliage. Its green leaves are often tinged with white and follow the three-part trefoil shape. Dainty white flowers, often with a hint of pink, have a scruffy, tousled appearance.

Perks • I adore the look and fragrance of clover in grass, busy with humming honeybees. It's known as honeysuckle grass for good reason. It also provides a tasty meal for rabbits and other small animals.

Pitfalls • If you prefer an immaculate lawn, clover probably won't be your best friend. Hoeing and hand pulling are your best bets at eradication.

Did you know? • The chance of finding a mythical four-leaf clover is thought to be about 1 in 5,000.

Wild carrot (*Daucus carota*)

Author

* Flowers	June to August
* Foliage	Deciduous
* Height	1m
* Spread	50cm
* Preferred conditions	Sun, partial shade
* Origin	Europe, south-western Asia, northern Africa
* Toxicity	No reported toxicity
* Also known as	Bird's nest, Queen Anne's lace

How to spot • Wild carrot is another umbellifer, like cow parsley (*Anthriscus sylvestris*, p. 158), and the two do look quite similar. However, *Daucus carota* flowers later in summer and often displays a lilac tinge to its flowers. The forked bracts of leaves look quite similar in shape to the leaves of carrot and herb parsley and are often tinged with purple like the flowers. You're most likely to see it popping up in chalky soils, meadows and coastal areas, although it can be found throughout the countryside and in gardens.

Perks • Like cow parsley, wild carrot can spread, but it's also a wild alternative to similar frothy flowering umbels sold for a much dearer sum in garden centres. The flowers have a delicate beauty and draw in bees, butterflies, moths, and wasps.

Pitfalls • Although it is non-toxic, the plant can cause skin irritation.

Did you know? • Wild carrot is thought to be an early ancestor of the orange carrots that are a staple of the British diet.

Wild marjoram (*Origanum vulgare*)

* Flowers	June to September
* Foliage	Deciduous
* Height	1m
* Spread	1m
* Preferred conditions	Sun, partial shade
* Origin	Europe, northern Africa
* Toxicity	Toxic to cats and dogs
* Also known as	English marjoram, grove marjoram, pot marjoram, wild marjoram, wintersweet

Author

How to spot • The simplest way to identify wild marjoram is to lean in and give it a good sniff: if the fragrance reminds you of Italian restaurants, then you've likely found it. It is actually the same plant as the Italian herb oregano. The dark green leaves are small and have a rounded shape. In summer, fragrant pinkish-purple flower clusters form at the end of the plant's reddish stems.

Perks • Many people plant oregano, or other fragrant herbs, on purpose, so if you happen to spot wild marjoram on your plot without any effort on your part, I'd preheat the oven and start rolling out the pizza dough. Wild marjoram nectar is a favourite meal among bees, too.

Pitfalls • The plant can begin to look bedraggled without regular pruning. And as marjoram is poisonous to cats and dogs, it's best to plant it somewhere out of their reach.

Did you know? • This wildflower is common on chalky soils and grasslands, where the soil is alkaline.

Wood avens (*Geum urbanum*)

Bryony Bowie

*	**Flowers**	May to August
*	**Foliage**	Evergreen
*	**Height**	1m
*	**Spread**	50cm
*	**Preferred conditions**	Partial shade
*	**Origin**	Europe, Asia
*	**Toxicity**	No reported toxicity
*	**Also known as**	Blessed herb, city avens, clove root, colewort, herb bennet, St Benedict's herb, star of the earth, water flower

How to spot • As its name suggests, wood avens is fond of shady spaces, like woodlands and at the base of hedgerows. It's also commonly seen in areas of the garden that receive less sunlight. The plant has hairy, three-lobed leaves and bears small yellow flowers on slim stems that tend to droop very quickly. It's perhaps easiest to identify once flowers start to go to seed – you'll be able to spot reddish-bronze, round seed heads that resemble tiny pom poms. These are hooked, like burrs, so can attach easily to clothing and animals.

Perks • It won't win any medals for being the most visually interesting wild plant, but it does provide a vital food source for the caterpillars of the grizzled skipper butterfly, and its five-petalled yellow flowers have a dainty charm. It is particularly suited to wildlife gardens and meadows.

Pitfalls • Wood avens is most likely an uninvited guest in a shady border, where it can spread via its underground stems. Weeding out the plant with a fork, roots and all, before it sets seed is probably your best bet at control.

Did you know? • The vernacular name herb bennet is related to benediction – the plant once held symbolic value for Christians, with its trefoil leaves said to represent the holy trinity.

Yarrow (*Achillea millefolium*)

Author

✳	**Flowers**	June to November
✳	**Foliage**	Deciduous
✳	**Height**	50cm
✳	**Spread**	50cm
✳	**Preferred conditions**	Sun
✳	**Origin**	Europe, Asia
✳	**Toxicity**	Toxic to cats, dogs and horses
✳	**Also known as**	Arrow-root, bloodwort, devil's nettle, greenarrow, hundred-leaved grass, lace plant, milfoil, nosebleed, nose pepper, old man's pepper, sanguinary, savoury tea, sneezewort, soldier's woundwort, thousand-leaf, thousand-seal, thousand weed, yellow

How to spot • Find yarrow in lawns, meadows, and other grassy areas, where you'll notice its flat white flowers and soft, feathery foliage. The clusters of flowers make it look a bit like an umbellifer, such as cow parsley (p. 158), but it is much smaller in stature. Each flower has five petals.

Perks • This member of the daisy family is known for improving poor soil and can be used to make homemade fertiliser for plants. And its flowers are regarded as desirable: cultivated forms with pink or yellow flowers are widely available for garden borders, where they spread easily.

Pitfalls • However, it can quickly spread in lawns on chalky soils, so some will prefer to remove it. It is also poisonous to several animal species.

Did you know? • In Greek mythology, Achilles – who lends his name to the plant's scientific title – was said to have carried the plant with him into battle, relying on its medicinal properties to treat wounds sustained in war.

Useful vocabulary

Nature Uninterrupted Photography

1959 Weeds Act
An act of law that governs the spread of five injurious weeds in the UK.

1981 Wildlife and Countryside Act
An act of law designed to protect various wildlife, habitats and plants in the UK.

Acid soil
Soil with a pH value of less than 7.

Aerial roots
Roots that grow above the ground.

Alkaline soil
Soil with a pH value above 7.

Aphids
Small insects, also known as blackfly or greenfly, which feed on plants by sucking out their sap.

Annual
A plant that germinates, flowers, sets seeds and dies over the course of one growing season.

Bedding plant
A fast-growing annual plant sold en masse in garden centres in spring.

Biennial
A plant that takes two years to complete its cycle of germination, flowering, setting seed and death.

Bolt
When a plant produces a flowering stem and goes to seed, usually when under stress.

Bract
A small and leaf-like structure positioned beneath a flower.

Chalky soil
Shallow, stony, alkaline soil that dries out quickly and is rich in chalky sediment.

Chlorophyll
The green pigment found in plants.

Clay soil
Sticky, dense, nutrient-rich soil, cracking in hot weather.

Corolla
Collective section of petals at the centre of a flower.

Cultivar
A variety of plant that has been produced by humans as the result of selective breeding.

Deadheading
The process of removing faded flowers from plants to encourage further flowering.

Deciduous
A plant that sheds its leaves at the end of the growing season (usually in autumn).

Dividing plants/division
The process of digging up and splitting a plant into sections, which are then replanted.

Evergreen
A plant that keeps its living leaves throughout the winter.

Floret
One of many small flowers that make up a flower head.

Frost pocket
A small, low area, hollow or valley more susceptible to frosts.

Germinate
To begin to grow from seed.

Grey mould
A common plant fungal disease that causes a greyish-brown mould to form and the decay of plant tissue.

Ground cover
Low-growing, spreading plants that cover bare soil and outcompete other plants and weeds in the same area.

Herbaceous perennial
A soft, non-woody plant with stems that die back over winter.

Leaflets
The leaf-like sections of a plant that collectively make up a leaf.

Lobed leaves or foliage
Leaves or foliage with deeply indented margins.

Naturalised
When a plant that is not native to a country or region adapts to a new environment and spreads widely, sometimes in an uncontrolled manner.

Neutral soil
Soil with a pH value of 7.

Palmately divided leaves or foliage; palmate
A leaf in the shape of an open hand, with lobes radiating from a central point.

Panicle
A loose, branching cluster of flowers, often in the shape of a cone.

Perennial
A plant that lives for more than two years and returns year after year, often dying back completely in the winter before re-emerging in spring.

Pinnately divided leaves or foliage; pinnate
Leaves are found on either side of a central stem, like a feather.

Poor soil
Soil lacking in nutrients or drainage, preferred by some weeds.

Powdery mildew
A common fungal disease of plants, identifiable from grey or white blemishes on the foliage or flowers.

Pruning
The removal of some parts of a plant, often woody stems, to improve its condition, shape and performance.

Rhizome
A horizontal, underground, spreading stem or root.

Sandy soil
Light, dry, acidic soil often lacking in nutrients.

Schedule 9
Part of the 1981 Wildlife and Countryside Act, which governs the spread of non-native invasive plants already established in the UK.

Seed head
A seed-containing part of a plant that forms following flowering or fruiting.

Self-seeder
A plant that spreads its seeds freely by various means (wind, birds, explosive seed pods) without the intervention of humans.

Semi-evergreen
Plants that lose their foliage for only a short period of the year.

Serrated leaves or foliage
Leaves with notched edges, resembling the teeth of a saw.

Shrub
A perennial woody plant, usually smaller than a tree.

Spp.
This botanical abbreviation is used as shorthand for multiple species.

Stamen
The male, reproductive element of a flower, normally visible as a thin stem and pollen-producing anther.

Trefoil leaves or foliage; trifoliate
Leaves with three distinct leaflets, as a clover.

Umbel or umbellifer
A flat-topped or rounded cluster of flowers where individual flower stalks extend from the same point.

Variegated
Leaves bearing more than one colour (often green and yellow).

Vine weevil
An insect that feeds on many garden plants.

Further resources

Several resources were helpful references in the writing of this book and should provide further inspiration for plant identification.

Books

Ary, S., Gregory, M. (Authors), Nicholson, B.E., (Illustrator), *The Oxford Book of Wildflowers*, Oxford University Press, 1960.

Davis, Brian, *The Complete Guide to Garden Plants*, Grisewood & Dempsey, Ltd, 1989.

Hamilton, Geoff, *Geoff Hamilton's Cottage Gardens*, BBC Books, 1997. Hessayon, Dr D.G., *The Tree & Shrub Expert*, PBI Publications, 1991.

Mabey, Richard, *Weeds: The Story of Outlaw Plants*, Profile Books, 2012.

Mendelson, Charlotte, *Rhapsody in Green*, Octopus Publishing Group, 2016.

Oudolf, Piet and Gerritsen, Henk, *Dream Plants for the Natural Garden*, Frances Lincoln Limited, 2013.

Proctor, Rob, *Antique Flowers: Perennials*, Cassell Illustrated, 1990.

Richardson, Rosamund, *Britain's Wildflowers*, National Trust Books, 2017.

Roth, Sally, *Weeds: Friend or Foe?*, Carroll & Brown Publishers Ltd, 2001.

Wallington, Jack, *Wild About Weeds: Garden Design with Rebel Plants*, Orion, 2019.

Websites

britannica.com/browse/Plants gardenfocused.co.uk
PlantSnap (mobile app available on Apple and Android Store), plantsnap.com
RHS.org.uk/plants

About the author

Louise Burfitt is a writer and translator. Born in London, she now lives in a small village near Oxford. She enjoys growing flowers, fruit and vegetables in her garden, on the allotment and as a volunteer with therapeutic gardening charity Restore. She is especially interested in the benefits of gardening for physical and mental health, and about widening accessibility to gardening.

Ashley Garrels

Acknowledgements

Writing a book, it turns out, is much like tending to a patch of soil. It takes patience and planning, and at the very moment you think you have finished and can enjoy a cup of tea and a sit-down, you think of something else that needs doing! Both endeavours are hugely enjoyable and both can require a huge investment of time and effort. Consequently, I am very grateful for the lovely enthusiasm and steadying support of much-loved friends and family (too many to list by name, but much appreciated) during the writing process as well as those who provided a listening ear, requested favourite plants as inclusions, and provided beautiful photographs.

Special personal mentions must go to the following:
Ashley Garrels, thank you for my author portrait! Just like you always promised.

Bryony Bowie, without whom this book would be little more than the sum of its parts. Thank you for your meticulous attention to detail, provision of allotment tea and snacks, for your plant-hunting vigour and unparalleled proofreading skills.

Eleanor Burfitt, thank you for the simply beautiful photographs you have contributed to this book, for all of the walks to Eastcote House Gardens (and beyond), and for making life more fun wherever you go.

Fred Burfitt. Thank you for being my first introduction to the wonder of a homegrown garden. From popping Busy Lizzies under the verandah to passing down your love of dahlias and homegrown tomatoes, so many of my childhood memories are found in the garden with you, Jane, Jenny and Little G.

Gail Jenkins & David Pocock, thanks for letting me photograph your enchanting garden - in all its high summer glory. It's one of my favourite places.

Laurent, Sophie & Jon at Restore as well as the many members and staff I am lucky enough to garden and learn alongside there - it is a true joy to be part of our community and a highlight of my week.

Matthew Pocock, thank you for carrying the compost, digging our Oxfordshire clay soil, and indulging my plantswoman antics with humour and aplomb. Thanks, most of all, for your unwavering belief in me.

Melanie & Nick Burfitt, thank you for the beautiful haven that is the Crescent garden. The climbing white roses are my favourite. Thanks for nurturing my interest in books and words.

Piers Harrington, when we first met I was astonished by your knowledge of plants. I still am! But you've taught me well. The seeds of this book were planted, perhaps, on those long walks beside the Danube a decade ago where you'd point out flora and fauna with delight and abandon.

And on the publishing side, I also extend heartfelt thanks to the following:

Kate Bohdanowicz, for initially contacting me about writing this book.

Janet Brookes, for production prowess and being a delight to communicate with.

Charlotte Mitchell, for publicity input and, equally, being lovely to work with.

Paul Middleton & Carol Trow, for their valuable copy edits, which have improved this book greatly.

You, the reader! Thank you for reading. I hope this book meets you where you're at and, above all, relays what I believe to be an essential truth: plants are for everyone.

Index